The Selected Works of
AUDRE LORDE

ALSO BY AUDRE LORDE

Poetry

The First Cities

Cables to Rage

From a Land Where Other People Live

New York Head Shop and Museum

Coal

Between Our Selves

The Black Unicorn

Chosen Poems: Old and New

Our Dead Behind Us

Undersong: Chosen Poems Old and New Revised

The Marvelous Arithmetics of Distance: Poems 1987–1992

The Collected Poems of Audre Lorde

Prose

The Cancer Journals

Uses of the Erotic: The Erotic as Power

Zami: A New Spelling of My Name

Sister Outsider: Essays and Speeches

A Burst of Light: Essays

I Am Your Sister:

Collected and Unpublished Writings of Audre Lorde

The Selected Works of

AUDRE LORDE

Edited and with an Introduction by
Roxane Gay

W. W. NORTON & COMPANY
Independent Publishers Since 1923

For information about permission to reproduce selections from this book,
write to Permissions, W. W. Norton & Company, Inc., 500 Fifth Avenue,
New York, NY 10110

For information about special discounts for bulk purchases, please contact
W. W. Norton Special Sales at specialsales@wwnorton.com or 800-233-4830

Manufacturing by LSC Communications, Harrisonburg
Book design by Lisa Buckley Design
Production manager: Lauren Abbate

Library of Congress Cataloging-in-Publication Data

Names: Lorde, Audre, author. | Gay, Roxane, editor.
Title: The selected works of Audre Lorde / edited and with an introduction
    by Roxane Gay.
Description: First edition. | New York, NY : W. W. Norton & Company,
    [2020] | Includes index.
Identifiers: LCCN 2020020850 | ISBN 9781324004615 (paperback) |
    ISBN 9781324004622 (epub)
Classification: LCC PS3562.O75 A6 2020 | DDC 814/.54—dc23
LC record available at https://lccn.loc.gov/2020020850

W. W. Norton & Company, Inc., 500 Fifth Avenue, New York, N.Y. 10110
www.wwnorton.com

W. W. Norton & Company Ltd., 15 Carlisle Street, London W1D 3BS

6 7 8 9 0

Contents

Introduction

Roxane Gay

There is this thing that happens, all too often, when a black woman is being introduced in a professional setting. Her accomplishments tend to be diminished. The introducer might laugh awkwardly, rushing through whatever impoverished remarks they have prepared. Rarely do they do the necessary research to offer any sense of whom they are introducing. The black woman is spoken of in terms of anecdote rather than accomplishment. She is referred to as sassy on Twitter, maybe, or as a lover of bacon, random tidbits bearing no relation to the reasons why she is in that professional setting. Whenever this happens to me or I witness it happening to another black woman, I turn to Audre Lorde. I wonder how Lorde would respond to such a micro-aggression because in her prescient writings she demonstrated, time and again, a remarkable and necessary ability to stand up for herself, her intellectual prowess and that of all black women, with power and grace. She recognized the importance of speaking up because silence would not protect her or anyone. She recognized that there would never be a perfect time to speak up because, "while we wait in silence for that final luxury of fearlessness, the weight of that silence will choke us."

In 1979, for example, Audre Lorde wrote a letter to Mary Daly, and when Daly did not respond to her missive Lorde made her entreaty an open letter. Lorde was primarily concerned with the erasure of black women in Daly's *Gyn/Ecology*, a manifesto urging women toward a more radical feminism. In her open letter, Lorde wrote, "So the question arises in my mind, Mary, do you ever really read the work of Black women? Did you ever read my words, or did you merely finger through them for quotations which you thought might valuably support an already conceived idea concerning some old and distorted connection between us? This is not a rhetorical question." The letter is both gracious and incisive. What Lorde is really demanding of Daly and white feminists more broadly is for them to seriously engage with and acknowledge black women's intellectual labor.

In the thirty years since Lorde wrote that open letter, black women have continued to implore white women to recognize and engage with their intellectual contributions and the material realities of their lives. They have asked white women to acknowledge that, as Lorde also wrote in her open letter to Daly, "The oppression of women knows no ethnic nor racial boundaries, true, but that does not mean it is identical within those differences." One of the hallmarks of Lorde's prose and poetry is her willingness to recognize, acknowledge, and honor the lived realities of women—not only those who share her subject position but also those who do not. Her thinking always embodied what we now know as intersectionality and did so long before intersectionality became a defining feature of contemporary feminism in word if not in deed.

Lorde never grappled with only one aspect of identity. She was as concerned with class, gender, and sexuality as she was with race. She held these concerns and did so with care because she valued community and the diversity of the people who were part of any given community. She valued the differences between us as strengths rather than weaknesses. Doing this was of particular urgency, because to her mind, "The future of our earth may depend upon the ability of all women to identify and develop new definitions of power and new patterns of relating across difference."

But how do you best represent a significant, in all senses of the word, body of work? This is the question that has consumed me as I assembled this Audre Lorde reader. Lorde is a towering figure in the world of letters, at least for me. I first encountered her writing in my early twenties, as a young black queer woman. She was the first writer I ever read who lived and loved the way I did and also looked like me. She was a beacon, a guiding light. And she was far more than that because her prose and poetry astonished me—intelligent, fierce, powerful, sensual, provocative, indelible.

When I read her books, I underlined and annotated avidly. I whispered her intimately crafted turns of phrase, enjoying the sound and feel of them in my mouth, on my tongue. Lorde was the first writer who actively demonstrated for me that a writer could be intensely concerned with the inner and outer lives of black queer women, that our experiences could be the center instead of relegated to the periphery. She wrote beyond the white gaze and imagined a black reality that did not subvert itself to the cultural norms dictated by whiteness. She valorized the body as much as she valorized the mind. She valorized nurturing as much as she valorized holding people accountable for their actions, calling out people and practices that decentered the black queer woman's experience and knowledge. Most importantly, she prioritized the collective because, "without community there is no liberation, only the most vulnerable and temporary armistice between an individual and her oppression." As a reader, it is gratifying to see the legacy Lorde has created and to see the genealogy of her work in the writing of the women who have followed in her footsteps. Without Lorde's essay "The Uses of Anger," we might never have known Claudia Rankine's manifesto of poetic prose, *Citizen*.

In one of her most fiery essays, "The Master's Tools Will Never Dismantle the Master's House," Lorde asks, "What does it mean when tools of a racist patriarchy are used to examine the fruits of that same patriarchy," and quickly answers her own question. "It means that only the most narrow perimeters of change are possible and allowable." Lorde gave these remarks in 1979 after being invited to an academic conference where there was only one panel with a black feminist or lesbian perspective and only two black women presenters. Forty years later, such meager representation is still an issue in many supposedly feminist and inclusive spaces. The essay is pointed, identifying pernicious issues marginalized people face in certain oppressive spaces—having to be the sole representative of their subject position, having to use their intellectual and emotional labor to address oppression instead of any of their other intellectual interests as if the marginalized are only equipped to talk about their marginalization.

This is a reality we often lose sight of when we surrender to assimilationist ideas about social change. There is, for example, a strain of feminism that believes if only women act like men, we will achieve the equality we seek. Lorde asks us to do the more difficult and radical work of imagining what our realities might look like if masculinity were not the ideal to which we aspire, if heterosexuality were not the ideal to which we aspire, if whiteness were not the ideal to which we aspire.

In Lorde's body of work, we see her defying this idea of the dominant culture as the default, this idea that she should only write about her oppression, but while doing so she never abandons her subject position. She is empathetic, curious, critical, intuitive. She is as open about her weaknesses as she is about her strengths. She is an exemplar of public intellectualism who is as relevant in this century as she was in the last.

We are rather attached to the notion of truth as singular, but the best writing reminds us that truth is complex and subjective. The best writing reminds us that we need not relegate the truth to the narrow perimeters of right and wrong, black and white, good and evil. I have thought about how narrow the perimeters of change really are when we insist on using the master's tools to dismantle the master's house. This narrow brand of thinking has only intensified since the 2016 presidential election, when Donald Trump was elected. Whatever progress it seemed like we were making during the Obama era has retracted sharply, painfully. We live in a very fractured time, one where difference has become weaponized, demonized, and where discourse demands allegiance to extremes instead of nuanced points of view. We live in a time where the president of the United States flouts all conventions of the office, decorum, and decency. Police brutality persists, unabated. Women share their experiences with sexual harassment or violence but rarely receive any kind of justice.

It seems like things have only gotten worse since the height of Lorde's career when she was writing about the very things we continue to deal with—the place of women and, more specifically, black women in the world, what it means to raise black girls and boys in a world that will not welcome them, what it means to live in a world so harshly stratified by class, what it means to live in a vulnerable body, what it means to live. There are very few voices for women and even fewer voices for black women, speaking from the center of consciousness, from the *I am* out to the *we are*, but Lorde was, throughout her storied career, one such voice. In her poem "Power," Lorde wrote about a white police officer who murdered a ten-year-old black boy and was acquitted by a jury of eleven of his peers and one black woman who succumbed to the will of those peers. She captured the rage of such injustice and how futile it feels to try and fight such injustice, but she also demonstrated that even in the face of futility, silence is never an option.

A great deal of Lorde's writing was committed to articulating her worldview in service of the greater good. She crafted lyrical manifestos. The essay "Poetry Is Not a Luxury" made the case for the importance of poetry, arguing that poetry "is a vital necessity of our existence. It forms the quality of light within which we predicate our hopes and dreams toward survival and change, first made into language, then into idea, then into more tangible action." In "Uses of the Erotic: The Erotic as Power," Lorde examines women using their erotic power to benefit themselves instead of benefiting men. She notes that women are often vilified for their erotic power and treated as inferior. She suggests that we can rethink and reframe this paradigm. This is what is so remarkable about Lorde's writing—how she encourages women to understand weaknesses as strengths. She writes, "As women, we need to examine the ways in which our world can be truly different. I am speaking here of the necessity for reassessing the quality of all aspects of our lives and our work, and how we move toward and through them." In this, she offers an expansive definition of the erotic, one that goes well beyond the carnal to encompass a wide range of sensate experiences.

Rethinking and reframing paradigms is a recurring theme in Lorde's writing. As the child of immigrants who came to the United States for their American dream only to have that dream shattered by the Great Depression, Lorde understood the nuances of oppression from an early age. It was poetry that gave her the language to make sense of that oppression and to resist it, and she was a prolific poet with several collections to her name including *The First Cities*, *Cables to Rage*, *From a Land Where Other People Live*, *Coal*, and *The Black Unicorn*.

Her work took other forms—teaching, cofounding Kitchen Table: Women of Color Press, public speaking, and a range of advocacy efforts for women, lesbians, and black people. During her time in Germany, she gave rise to the Afro-German movement—helping black German women use their voices to join the sisterhood she valued so dearly. She also demanded that white German women confront their whiteness, even when it made them defensive or uncomfortable. In an essay about Lorde's time in Germany, Dagmar Schultz wrote that "many white women learned to be more conscious of their privileges and more responsible in the use of their power."

Lorde was not constrained by boundaries. She combined the personal and the political, the spiritual and the secular. As an academic she fearlessly wrote about the sensual and the sexual even though the academy has long disdained such interests. Her erotic life was as valuable as her intellectual life and she was unabashed in making this known.

This refusal to be constrained was notably apparent in *Zami: A New Spelling of My Name*, which she called a "biomythography." Biographer Alexis De Veaux describes *Zami*, in her definitive biography of Lorde, *Warrior Poet: A Biography of Audre Lorde*, as a book that "recovers from existing male-dominated literary genres (history, mythology, autobiography, and fiction) whatever was inextricably female, female-centered." In *Zami* and much of her other work, Lorde expressed the radical idea that black women could hold the center, be the center, and she was unwavering in this belief.

At her most vulnerable, Lorde gave the world some of her most powerful writing with her work in *The Cancer Journals*, which chronicled her life with breast cancer and having a double mastectomy. "But it is that very difference which I wish to affirm, because I have lived it, and survived it, and wish to share that strength with other women. If we are to translate the silence surrounding breast cancer into language and action against this scourge, then the first step is that women with mastectomies must become visible to each other." With these words, she assumed as much control as she could over a body succumbing to disease and a public narrative that, until then, allowed a singular narrative about what it meant to live with illness. She made herself visible and gave other women permission to make themselves visible in a world that would prefer that they disappear, stay silent.

In all of her writing, Audre Lorde offers us language to articulate how we might heal our fractured sociopolitical climate. She gives us instructions for making tools with which we can dismantle the houses of our oppressors. She remakes language with which we can revel in our sensual and sexual selves. She forges a space within which we can hold ourselves and each other accountable to both our needs and the greater good.

Anthologies like this are so very necessary because, all too often, people misappropriate the words and ideas of black women. They do so selectively, using the parts that serve their aims, and abandoning those parts that don't. People will, for example, parrot Lorde's ideas about dismantling the master's house without taking into account the context from which Lorde crafted those ideas. Lorde is such a brilliant and eloquent writer; she has such a way of shaping language that of course people want to repeat her words to their own ends. But her work is far more than something pretty to parrot. In this collection of Lorde's prose and poetry, you will be able to appreciate the grace, power, and fierce intelligence of her writing, to understand where she was writing from and why, and to bear witness to all the unforgettable ways she made herself, and all black women, gloriously visible.

PROSE

Poetry Is Not a Luxury

The quality of light by which we scrutinize our lives has direct bearing upon the product which we live, and upon the changes which we hope to bring about through those lives. It is within this light that we form those ideas by which we pursue our magic and make it realized. This is poetry as illumination, for it is through poetry that we give name to those ideas which are—until the poem—nameless and formless, about to be birthed, but already felt. That distillation of experience from which true poetry springs births thought as dream births concept, as feeling births idea, as knowledge births (precedes) understanding.

As we learn to bear the intimacy of scrutiny and to flourish within it, as we learn to use the products of that scrutiny for power within our living, those fears which rule our lives and form our silences begin to lose their control over us.

For each of us as women, there is a dark place within, where hidden and growing our true spirit rises, "beautiful/and tough as chestnut/stanchions against (y)our nightmare of weakness/"* and of impotence.

These places of possibility within ourselves are dark because

---

* From "Black Mother Woman," first published in *From A Land Where Other People Live* (Broadside Press, Detroit, 1973), and collected in *Chosen Poems: Old and New* (W. W. Norton & Company, New York, 1982), p. 53.

they are ancient and hidden; they have survived and grown strong through that darkness. Within these deep places, each one of us holds an incredible reserve of creativity and power, of unexamined and unrecorded emotion and feeling. The woman's place of power within each of us is neither white nor surface; it is dark, it is ancient, and it is deep.

When we view living in the european mode only as a problem to be solved, we rely solely upon our ideas to make us free, for these were what the white fathers told us were precious.

But as we come more into touch with our own ancient, non-european consciousness of living as a situation to be experienced and interacted with, we learn more and more to cherish our feelings, and to respect those hidden sources of our power from where true knowledge and, therefore, lasting action comes.

At this point in time, I believe that women carry within ourselves the possibility for fusion of these two approaches so necessary for survival, and we come closest to this combination in our poetry. I speak here of poetry as a revelatory distillation of experience, not the sterile word play that, too often, the white fathers distorted the word *poetry* to mean—in order to cover a desperate wish for imagination without insight.

For women, then, poetry is not a luxury. It is a vital necessity of our existence. It forms the quality of the light within which we predicate our hopes and dreams toward survival and change, first made into language, then into idea, then into more tangible action. Poetry is the way we help give name to the nameless so it can be thought. The farthest horizons of our hopes and fears are cobbled by our poems, carved from the rock experiences of our daily lives.

As they become known to and accepted by us, our feelings and the honest exploration of them become sanctuaries and spawning grounds for the most radical and daring of ideas.

They become a safe-house for that difference so necessary to change and the conceptualization of any meaningful action. Right now, I could name at least ten ideas I would have found intolerable or incomprehensible and frightening, except as they came after dreams and poems. This is not idle fantasy, but a disciplined attention to the true meaning of "it feels right to me." We can train ourselves to respect our feelings and to transpose them into a language so they can be shared. And where that language does not yet exist, it is our poetry which helps to fashion it. Poetry is not only dream and vision; it is the skeleton architecture of our lives. It lays the foundations for a future of change, a bridge across our fears of what has never been before.

Possibility is neither forever nor instant. It is not easy to sustain belief in its efficacy. We can sometimes work long and hard to establish one beachhead of real resistance to the deaths we are expected to live, only to have that beachhead assaulted or threatened by those canards we have been socialized to fear, or by the withdrawal of those approvals that we have been warned to seek for safety. Women see ourselves diminished or softened by the falsely benign accusations of childishness, of nonuniversality, of changeability, of sensuality. And who asks the question: Am I altering your aura, your ideas, your dreams, or am I merely moving you to temporary and reactive action? And even though the latter is no mean task, it is one that must be seen within the context of a need for true alteration of the very foundations of our lives.

The white fathers told us: I think, therefore I am. The Black mother within each of us—the poet—whispers in our dreams: I feel, therefore I can be free. Poetry coins the language to express and charter this revolutionary demand, the implementation of that freedom.

However, experience has taught us that action in the now is also necessary, always. Our children cannot dream unless they live, they cannot live unless they are nourished, and who else will feed them the real food without which their dreams will be no different from ours? "If you want us to change the world someday, we at least have to live long enough to grow up!" shouts the child.

Sometimes we drug ourselves with dreams of new ideas. The head will save us. The brain alone will set us free. But there are no new ideas still waiting in the wings to save us as women, as human. There are only old and forgotten ones, new combinations, extrapolations and recognitions from within ourselves—along with the renewed courage to try them out. And we must constantly encourage ourselves and each other to attempt the heretical actions that our dreams imply, and so many of our old ideas disparage. In the forefront of our move toward change, there is only poetry to hint at possibility made real. Our poems formulate the implications of ourselves, what we feel within and dare make real (or bring action into accordance with), our fears, our hopes, our most cherished terrors.

For within living structures defined by profit, by linear power, by institutional dehumanization, our feelings were not meant to survive. Kept around as unavoidable adjuncts or pleasant pastimes, feelings were expected to kneel to thought as women were expected to kneel to men. But women have survived. As poets. And there are no new pains. We have felt them all already. We have hidden that fact in the same place where we have hidden our power. They surface in our dreams, and it is our dreams that point the way to freedom. Those dreams are made realizable through our poems that give us the strength and courage to see, to feel, to speak, and to dare.

If what we need to dream, to move our spirits most deeply

and directly toward and through promise, is discounted as a luxury, then we give up the core—the fountain—of our power, our womanness; we give up the future of our worlds.

For there are no new ideas. There are only new ways of making them felt—of examining what those ideas feel like being lived on Sunday morning at 7 A.M., after brunch, during wild love, making war, giving birth, mourning our dead—while we suffer the old longings, battle the old warnings and fears of being silent and impotent and alone, while we taste new possibilities and strengths.

The Transformation of Silence into Language and Action

I have come to believe over and over again that what is most important to me must be spoken, made verbal and shared, even at the risk of having it bruised or misunderstood. That the speaking profits me, beyond any other effect. I am standing here as a Black lesbian poet, and the meaning of all that waits upon the fact that I am still alive, and might not have been. Less than two months ago I was told by two doctors, one female and one male, that I would have to have breast surgery, and that there was a 60 to 80 percent chance that the tumor was malignant. Between that telling and the actual surgery, there was a three-week period of the agony of an involuntary reorganization of my entire life. The surgery was completed, and the growth was benign.

But within those three weeks, I was forced to look upon myself and my living with a harsh and urgent clarity that has left me still shaken but much stronger. This is a situation faced by many women, by some of you here today. Some of what I experienced during that time has helped elucidate for me much of what I feel concerning the transformation of silence into language and action.

In becoming forcibly and essentially aware of my mortality, and of what I wished and wanted for my life, however short it might be, priorities and omissions became strongly etched in a merciless light, and what I most regretted were my silences. Of what had I ever been afraid? To question or to speak as I believed could have meant pain, or death. But we all hurt in so many different ways, all the time, and pain will either change or end. Death, on the other hand, is the final silence. And that might be coming quickly, now, without regard for whether I had ever spoken what needed to be said, or had only betrayed myself into small silences, while I planned someday to speak, or waited for someone else's words. And I began to recognize a source of power within myself that comes from the knowledge that while it is most desirable not to be afraid, learning to put fear into a perspective gave me great strength.

I was going to die, if not sooner then later, whether or not I had ever spoken myself. My silences had not protected me. Your silence will not protect you. But for every real word spoken, for every attempt I had ever made to speak those truths for which I am still seeking, I had made contact with other women while we examined the words to fit a world in which we all believed, bridging our differences. And it was the concern and caring of all those women which gave me strength and enabled me to scrutinize the essentials of my living.

The women who sustained me through that period were Black and white, old and young, lesbian, bisexual, and heterosexual, and we all shared a war against the tyrannies of silence. They all gave me a strength and concern without which I could not have survived intact. Within those weeks of acute fear came the knowledge—within the war we are all waging with the forces of death, subtle and otherwise, conscious or not—I am not only a casualty, I am also a warrior.

What are the words you do not yet have? What do you need to say? What are the tyrannies you swallow day by day and attempt to make your own, until you will sicken and die of them, still in silence? Perhaps for some of you here today, I am the face of one of your fears. Because I am woman, because I am Black, because I am lesbian, because I am myself—a Black woman warrior poet doing my work—come to ask you, are you doing yours?

And of course I am afraid, because the transformation of silence into language and action is an act of self-revelation, and that always seems fraught with danger. But my daughter, when I told her of our topic and my difficulty with it, said, "Tell them about how you're never really a whole person if you remain silent, because there's always that one little piece inside you that wants to be spoken out, and if you keep ignoring it, it gets madder and madder and hotter and hotter, and if you don't speak it out one day it will just up and punch you in the mouth from the inside."

In the cause of silence, each of us draws the face of her own fear—fear of contempt, of censure, or some judgment, or recognition, of challenge, of annihilation. But most of all, I think, we fear the visibility without which we cannot truly live. Within this country where racial difference creates a constant, if unspoken, distortion of vision, Black women have on one hand always been highly visible, and so, on the other hand, have been rendered invisible through the depersonalization of racism. Even within the women's movement, we have had to fight, and still do, for that very visibility which also renders us most vulnerable, our Blackness. For to survive in the mouth of this dragon we call america, we have had to learn this first and most vital lesson—

that we were never meant to survive. Not as human beings. And neither were most of you here today, Black or not. And that visibility which makes us most vulnerable is that which also is the source of our greatest strength. Because the machine will try to grind you into dust anyway, whether or not we speak. We can sit in our corners mute forever while our sisters and our selves are wasted, while our children are distorted and destroyed, while our earth is poisoned; we can sit in our safe corners mute as bottles, and we will still be no less afraid.

In my house this year we are celebrating the feast of Kwanza, the African-american festival of harvest which begins the day after Christmas and lasts for seven days. There are seven principles of Kwanza, one for each day. The first principle is Umoja, which means unity, the decision to strive for and maintain unity in self and community. The principle for yesterday, the second day, was Kujichagulia—self-determination—the decision to define ourselves, name ourselves, and speak for ourselves, instead of being defined and spoken for by others. Today is the third day of Kwanza, and the principle for today is Ujima—collective work and responsibility—the decision to build and maintain ourselves and our communities together and to recognize and solve our problems together.

Each of us is here now because in one way or another we share a commitment to language and to the power of language, and to the reclaiming of that language which has been made to work against us. In the transformation of silence into language and action, it is vitally necessary for each one of us to establish or examine her function in that transformation and to recognize her role as vital within that transformation.

For those of us who write, it is necessary to scrutinize not only the truth of what we speak, but the truth of that language by which we speak it. For others, it is to share and spread also those words that are meaningful to us. But primarily for us all, it is necessary to teach by living and speaking those truths which we believe and know beyond understanding. Because in this way alone we can survive, by taking part in a process of life that is creative and continuing, that is growth.

And it is never without fear—of visibility, of the harsh light of scrutiny and perhaps judgment, of pain, of death. But we have lived through all of those already, in silence, except death. And I remind myself all the time now that if I were to have been born mute, or had maintained an oath of silence my whole life long for safety, I would still have suffered, and I would still die. It is very good for establishing perspective.

And where the words of women are crying to be heard, we must each of us recognize our responsibility to seek those words out, to read them and share them and examine them in their pertinence to our lives. That we not hide behind the mockeries of separations that have been imposed upon us and which so often we accept as our own. For instance, "I can't possibly teach Black women's writing—their experience is so different from mine." Yet how many years have you spent teaching Plato and Shakespeare and Proust? Or another, "She's a white woman and what could she possibly have to say to me?" Or, "She's a lesbian, what would my husband say, or my chairman?" Or again, "This woman writes of her sons and I have no children." And all the other endless ways in which we rob ourselves of ourselves and each other.

We can learn to work and speak when we are afraid in the same way we have learned to work and speak when we are tired. For we have been socialized to respect fear more than our own needs for language and definition, and while we wait in silence for that final luxury of fearlessness, the weight of that silence will choke us.

The fact that we are here and that I speak these words is an attempt to break that silence and bridge some of those differences between us, for it is not difference which immobilizes us, but silence. And there are so many silences to be broken.

My Mother's Mortar

When I was growing up in my mother's house, there were spices you grated and spices you pounded, and whenever you pounded spice and garlic or other herbs, you used a mortar. Every West Indian woman worth her salt had her own mortar. Now if you lost or broke your mortar, of course, you could buy another one in the market over on Park Avenue, under the bridge, but those were usually Puerto Rican mortars, and even though they were made out of wood and worked exactly the same way, somehow they were never really as good as West Indian mortar[s]. Now where the best mortars came from I was never really sure, but I knew it must be in the vicinity of that amorphous and mystically perfect place called "home." "Home" was the West Indies, Grenada or Barbados to be exact, and whatever came from "home" was bound to be special.

My mother's mortar was a beautiful affair, quite at variance with most of her other possessions, and certainly with her projected public view of herself. It had stood, solid and elegant, on a shelf in the kitchen cabinet for as long as I can remember, and I loved it dearly.

The mortar was of a foreign fragrant wood, too dark for

cherry and too red for walnut. To my child's eyes, the outside was carved in an intricate and most enticing manner. There were rounded plums and oval indeterminate fruit, some long and fluted like a banana, others ovular and end-swollen like a ripe alligator pear. In between these were smaller rounded shapes like cherries, lying in batches against and around each other.

I loved to finger the hard roundness of the carved fruit, and the always surprising termination of the shapes as the carvings stopped at the rim and the bowl sloped abruptly downward, smoothly oval but suddenly businesslike. The heavy sturdiness of this useful wooden object always made me feel secure and somehow full; as if it conjured up from all the many different flavors pounded into the inside wall, visions of delicious feasts both once enjoyed and still to come.

The pestle was a slender tapering wand, fashioned from the same mysterious rose-deep wood, and fitted into the hand almost casually, familiarly. The actual shape reminded me of a summer crook-necked squash uncurled and slightly twisted. It could also have been an avocado, with the neck of the alligator pear elongated and the whole made businesslike and efficient for pounding, without ever losing the apparent soft firmness and the character of the fruit, which the wood suggested. It was slightly bigger at the grinding end than most pestles, and the widened curved end fitted into the bowl of the mortar easily. Long use and years of impact and grinding within the bowl's worn hollow had softened the very surface of the wooden pestle until a thin layer of split fibers coated the rounded end like a layer of velvet. A layer of the same velvety mashed wood lined the bottom inside the sloping bowl.

My mother did not particularly like to pound spice, and she looked upon the advent of powdered everything as a cook's boon. But there were some certain dishes that called for a particular savory blending of garlic, raw onion, and pepper, and souse was one of them.

For our mother's souse, it didn't matter what kind of meat was used. You could have hearts, or beef ends, or even chicken backs and gizzards when we were really poor. It was the pounded up saucy blend of herb[s] and spice[s] rubbed into the meat before it was left to stand so for a few hours before cooking that made that dish so special and unforgettable. But my mother had some very firm ideas about what she liked best to cook and about which were her favorite dishes, and souse was definitely not one of either.

On the very infrequent occasions that my mother would allow one of us three girls to choose a meal—as opposed to helping to prepare it, which was a daily routine—on those occasions my sisters would usually choose one of those proscribed dishes so dear to our hearts remembered from our relatives' tables, contraband, and so very rare in our house. They might ask for hot dogs, perhaps, smothered in ketchup sauce, or with crusty Boston-baked beans; or american chicken, breaded first and fried crispy the way the southern people did it; or creamed something-or-other that one of my sisters had tasted at school; what-have-you croquettes or anything fritters; or once even a daring outrageous request for slices of fresh watermelon, hawked from the back of a rickety wooden pickup truck with the southern road dust still on her slatted sides, from which a young bony Black man with a turned-around ballcap on his head would hang and half-yell, half-yodel—"Wahr—deeeeeee—mayyyyyyyy—lawnnnnnnnn."

There were many american dishes I longed for too, but on the one or two occasions a year that I got to choose a meal, I would always ask for souse. That way, I knew that I would get to use my mother's mortar, and this in itself was more treat for me than any of the forbidden foods.

Besides, if I really wanted hot dogs or anything croquettes badly enough, I could steal some money from my father's pocket and buy them in the school lunch[room].

"Mother, let's have souse," I'd say, and never even stop to think about it. The anticipated taste of the soft spicy meat had become inseparable in my mind from the tactile pleasures of using my mother's mortar.

"But what makes you think anybody can find time to mash up all that stuff?" my mother would cut her hawk-grey eyes at me from beneath their heavy black brows. "Among you children never stop to think, you know," and she'd turn back to whatever it was she had been doing. If she had just come from the office with my father, she might be checking the day's receipts, or she might be washing the endless piles of dirty linen that always seemed to issue from the rooming houses they managed.

"Oh, I'll pound the garlic, Mommy!" would be my next line in the script written by some ancient and secret hand, and off I'd go to the cabinet to get down the heavy wooden mortar and pestle.

I would get a head of garlic out from the garlic bottle in the icebox, and breaking off ten or twelve cloves from the head, I would carefully peel away the tissue lavender skin, slicing each stripped peg in half lengthwise. Then I would drop them piece by piece into the capacious waiting bowl of the mortar. Taking a slice from a small onion, I would put the rest aside, to be used later on over the meat, and cutting the slice into quarters, I would toss it into the mortar also. Next came the coarsely ground fresh black pepper, and then a lavish blanketing cover of salt over the whole. Last, if we had any, a few leaves from the top of a head of celery would be thrown in. My mother would sometimes add a slice of green pepper to be mashed in also, but I did not like the textures of the pepper skin under the pestle, and preferred to add it along with the sliced onion later on, leaving it all to sit over the seasoned and resting meat.

After all the ingredients were in the bowl of the mortar, I would fetch the pestle and placing it into the bowl, slowly rotate the shaft a few times, working it gently down through all the ingredients to mix them. Only then would I lift the pestle, and with one hand firmly pressed around the carved side of the mortar caressing the wooden fruit with my aromatic fingers, I would thrust sharply downward, feeling the shifting salt and the hard little pellets of garlic right up through the shaft of the wooden pestle. Up again, down, around, and up, so the rhythm would begin. The thud push rub rotate and up, repeated over and over; the muted thump of the pestle on the bed of grinding spice, as the salt and pepper absorbed the slowly yielded juices of the garlic and celery leaves and became moist; the mingling fragrances rising from the bowl of the mortar; the feeling of the pestle held between my fingers and the rounded fruit of the mortar's outside against my palm and curving fingers as I steadied it against my body; all these transported me into a world of scent and rhythm and movement and sound that grew more and more exciting as the ingredients liquefied.

Sometimes my mother would look over at me with that amused annoyance which passed for tenderness with her, and which was always such a welcome change for me from the furious annoyance which was so much more usual.

"What you think you making there, garlic soup? Enough, go get the meat now." And I would fetch the lamb hearts, for instance, from the icebox and begin to prepare them. Cutting away the hardened veins at the top of the smooth firm muscles,

I would divide each oval heart into four wedge-shaped pieces, and taking a bit of the spicy mash from the mortar with my fingertips, I would rub each piece with the savory mix. The pungent smell of garlic and onion and celery would envelop the kitchen.

The last day I ever pounded seasoning for souse was in the summer of my fourteenth year. It had been a fairly unpleasant summer, for me. I had just finished my first year in high school. Instead of being able to visit my newly found friends, all of whom lived in other parts of the city, I had had to accompany my mother on a round of doctors with whom she would have long whispered conversations that I was not supposed to listen to. Only a matter of the utmost importance could have kept her away from the office for so many mornings in a row. But my mother was concerned because I was fourteen and a half years old and had not yet menstruated. I had breasts but no period, and she was afraid there was "something wrong" with me. Yet, since she had never discussed this mysterious business of menstruation with me, I was certainly not supposed to know what all this whispering was about, even though it concerned my own body.

Of course, I knew as much as I could have possibly found out in those days from the hard-to-get books on the closed shelf behind the librarian's desk at the public library, where I had brought a forged note from home in order to be allowed to read them, sitting under the watchful eye of the librarian at a special desk reserved for that purpose.

Although not terribly informative, they were fascinating books, and used words like menses and ovulation and vagina.

But four years before, I had had to find out if I was going to become pregnant, because a boy from school much bigger than me had invited me up to the roof on my way home from the library and then threatened to break my glasses if I didn't let him stick his thing between my legs. And at that time I knew only that being pregnant had something to do with sex, and sex had something to do with that thin pencil-like thing and was in general nasty and not to be talked about by nice people, and I was afraid my mother might find out and what would she do to me then? I was not supposed to be looking at the mailboxes in the hallway of that house anyway, even though Doris was a girl in my class at St. Mark's who lived in that house and I was always so lonely in the summer, particularly that summer when I was ten.

So after I got home I washed myself up and lied about why I was late getting home from the library and got a whipping for being late. That must have been a hard summer for my parents at the office too, because that was the summer that I got a whipping for something or other almost every day between the 4th of July and Labor Day.

When I wasn't getting whippings, I hid out at the library on 135th Street and forged notes from my mother to get books from the closed shelf and read about sex and having babies and waited to become pregnant. None of the books were very clear to me about the relationship between having your period and having a baby, but they were all very clear about the relationship between penises and getting pregnant. Or maybe the confusion was all in my own mind, because I had always been a very fast but not a very careful reader.

So four years later, in my fourteenth year, I was a very scared little girl, still half-afraid that one of that endless stream of doctors would look up into my body and discover my four-year-old shame and say to my mother, "Aha! So that's what's wrong! Your daughter is about to become pregnant!"

On the other hand, if I let my mother know that I knew

what was happening and what these medical safaris were all about, I would have to answer her questions about how and wherefore I knew, since she hadn't told me, divulging in the process the whole horrible and self-incriminating story of forbidden books and forged library notes and rooftops and stairwell conversations.

A year after the rooftop incident, we moved farther uptown and I was transferred to a different school. The kids there seemed to know a lot more about sex than at St. Mark's, and in the eighth grade, I had stolen money and bought Adeline a pack of cigarettes and she had confirmed my bookish suspicions about how babies were made. My response to her graphic descriptions had been to think to myself—there obviously must be another way that Adeline doesn't know about, because my parents have children and I know they never did anything like that. But the basic principles were all there, and sure enough they were the same as I had gathered from *The Young People's Family Book.*

So in my fourteenth summer, on examining table after examining table, I kept my legs open and my mouth shut, and when I saw blood on my pants one hot July afternoon, I rinsed them out secretly in the bathroom and put them back on wet because I didn't know how to break the news to my mother that both her worries and mine were finally over. (All this time I had at least understood that having your period was a sign you were not pregnant.)

What then happened felt like a piece of an old and elaborate dance between my mother and me. She discovers finally, through a stain on the toilet seat left there on purpose by me as a mute announcement, what has taken place; she scolds, "Why didn't you tell me about all of this, now? It's nothing to get upset over, now you are a woman, not a child any more. Now you go over to the drugstore and ask the man for . . ."

I was just relieved the whole damn thing was over with. It's difficult to talk about double messages without having a twin tongue. But meanwhile all these nightmarish evocations and restrictions were being verbalized by my mother: "Now this means from now on you better watch your step and not be so friendly with every Tom Dick and Harry . . ." (which must have meant my staying late after school to talk with my girlfriends, because I did not even know any boys); and, "Now remember too, don't leave your soiled napkins wrapped up in newspaper hanging around on the bathroom floor where your father has to see them, not that it's anything shameful but all the same remember . . ."

Along with all of these admonitions, there was something else coming from my mother that I almost could not define. It was the lurking of that amused/annoyed brow-furrowed half-smile that passed as an intimate moment between my mother and me, and I really felt—all her nagging words to the contrary, or the more confusing—that something very good and satisfactory and pleasing to her had just happened, and that we were both pretending otherwise for some very wise and secret reasons which I would come to understand later as a reward if I handled myself properly. And then at the end of it all, my mother thrust the box of Kotex in its plain wrapper which I had fetched back from the drugstore with a sanitary belt at me, and said, "But look now what time it is already, I wonder what we're going to eat for supper tonight?" She waited. At first I didn't understand, but I quickly picked up the cue. I had seen the beef ends in the icebox that morning.

"Mommy, please let's have some souse—I'll pound the garlic." I dropped the box onto a kitchen chair and started to wash my hands in anticipation.

"Well, go put your business away first. What did I tell you

about leaving that lying around?" She wiped her hands from the washtub where she had been working and handed the plain wrapped box of Kotex back to me.

"I have to go out, I forgot to pick up tea at the store. Now make sure you rub the meat good."

When I came back into the kitchen, my mother had left. I moved toward the kitchen cabinet to fetch down the mortar and pestle. My body felt new and special and unfamiliar and suspect all at the same time.

I could feel bands of tension sweeping across my body back and forth like lunar winds across the moon's face. I felt the slight rubbing bulge of the cotton pad between my legs, and I smelled the warm delicate breadfruit smell rising up from the front of my print blouse that was my own womansmell, erotic, shameful, but secretly utterly delicious.

(Years afterward when I was grown, whenever I thought about the way I smelled that day, I would have a fantasy of my mother, her hands wiped dry from the washing, and her apron untied and laid neatly away, looking down upon me lying on the couch, and then slowly, thoroughly, our making love to each other.)

I took the mortar down, and smashed the cloves of garlic with the edge of its underside, to loosen the thin papery skins in a hurry. I sliced them and flung them into the mortar's bowl along with some black pepper and celery leaves. The white salt poured in, covering the garlic and black pepper and pale chartreuse celery fronds like a snowfall. I tossed in the onion and some bits of green pepper and reached for the pestle.

It slipped through my fingers and clattered to the floor, rolling around in a semicircle back and forth, until I bent to retrieve it. I grabbed the head of the wooden stick and straightened up, my ears ringing faintly. Without even wiping it,

I plunged the pestle into the bowl, feeling the blanket of salt give way, and the broken cloves of garlic just beneath. The downward thrust of the avocado-shaped wooden pestle slowed upon contact, rotated back and forth slowly, and then gently altered its rhythm to include an up and down beat. Back and forth, round, up and down, back, forth, round, round, up and down . . . There was a heavy fullness at the root of me that was exciting and dangerous.

As I continued to pound the spice, a vital connection seemed to establish itself between the muscles of my fingers curved tightly around the smooth pestle in its insistent downward motion, and the molten core of my body whose source emanated from a new ripe fullness just beneath the pit of my stomach. That invisible thread, taut and sensitive as a clitoris exposed, stretched through my curled fingers up my rounded brown arm into the moist reality of my armpits, whose warm sharp odor with a strange new overlay mixed with the ripe garlic smells from the mortar and the general sweat-heavy aromas of high summer.

The thread ran over my ribs and along my spine, tingling and singing, into a basin that was poised between my hips, now pressed against the low kitchen counter before which I stood, pounding spice. And within that basin was a tiding ocean of blood beginning to be made real and available to me for strength and information.

The jarring shocks of the velvet-lined pestle, striking the bed of spice, traveled up an invisible pathway along the thread into the center of me, and the harshness of the repeated impacts became increasingly more unbearable. The tidal basin suspended between my hips shuddered at each repetition of the strokes which now felt like assaults. Without my volition my downward thrusts of the pestle grew gentler and gentler until its velvety surface seemed almost to caress the liquefying mash at the bottom of the mortar.

The whole rhythm of my movements softened and elongated until, dreamlike, I stood, one hand tightly curved around the carved mortar, steadying it against the middle of my body; while my other hand, around the pestle, rubbed and pressed the moistening spice into readiness with a sweeping circular movement.

I hummed tunelessly to myself as I worked in the warm kitchen, thinking with relief about how simple my life had become now that I was a woman. The catalog of dire menstruation warnings from my mother passed out of my head. My body felt strong and full and open, yet captivated by the gentle motions of the pestle, and the rich smells filling the kitchen, and the fullness of the young summer heat.

I heard my mother's key in the lock.

She swept into the kitchen briskly, like a ship under full sail. There were tiny beads of sweat over her upper lip, and vertical creases between her brows.

"You mean to tell me no meat is ready?" My mother dropped her parcel of tea onto the table, and looking over my shoulder, sucked her teeth loudly in weary disgust. "What do you call yourself doing, now? You have all night to stand up there playing with the food? I go all the way to the store and back already and still you can't mash up a few pieces of garlic to season some meat? But you know how to do the thing better than this! Why you vex me so?"

She took the mortar and pestle out of my hands and started to grind vigorously. And there were still bits of garlic left at the bottom of the bowl.

"Now you do, so!" She brought the pestle down inside the bowl of the mortar with dispatch, crushing the last of the garlic. I heard the thump of wood brought down heavily upon wood, and I felt the harsh impact throughout my body, as if something had broken inside of me. Thump, thump, went the pestle, purposefully, up and down in the old familiar way.

"It was getting mashed, Mother," I dared to protest, turning away to the icebox. "I'll fetch the meat." I was surprised at my own brazenness in answering back.

But something in my voice interrupted my mother's efficient motions.

She ignored my implied contradiction, itself an act of rebellion strictly forbidden in our house. The thumping stopped.

"What's wrong with you, now? Are you sick? You want to go to your bed?"

"No, I'm all right, Mother."

But I felt her strong fingers on my upper arm, turning me around, her other hand under my chin as she peered into my face. Her voice softened.

"Is it your period making you so slow-down today?" She gave my chin a little shake, as I looked up into her hooded grey eyes, now becoming almost gentle. The kitchen felt suddenly oppressively hot and still, and I felt myself beginning to shake all over.

Tears I did not understand started from my eyes, as I realized that my old enjoyment of the bone-jarring way I had been taught to pound spice would feel different to me from now on, and also that in my mother's kitchen, there was only one right way to do anything. Perhaps my life had not become so simple, after all.

My mother stepped away from the counter and put her heavy arm around my shoulders. I could smell the warm herness rising from between her arm and her body, mixed with the smell of glycerine and rose-water, and the scent of her thick bun of hair.

"I'll finish up the food for supper." She smiled at me, and there was a tenderness in her voice and an absence of annoyance that was welcome, although unfamiliar.

"You come inside now and lie down on the couch and I'll make you a hot cup of tea."

Her arm across my shoulders was warm and slightly damp. I rested my head upon her shoulder, and realized with a shock of pleasure and surprise that I was almost as tall as my mother, as she led me into the cool darkened parlor.

Uses of the Erotic

The Erotic as Power

There are many kinds of power, used and unused, acknowledged or otherwise. The erotic is a resource within each of us that lies in a deeply female and spiritual plane, firmly rooted in the power of our unexpressed or unrecognized feeling. In order to perpetuate itself, every oppression must corrupt or distort those various sources of power within the culture of the oppressed that can provide energy for change. For women, this has meant a suppression of the erotic as a considered source of power and information within our lives.

We have been taught to suspect this resource, vilified, abused, and devalued within western society. On the one hand, the superficially erotic has been encouraged as a sign of female inferiority; on the other hand, women have been made to suffer and to feel both contemptible and suspect by virtue of its existence.

It is a short step from there to the false belief that only by the suppression of the erotic within our lives and consciousness can women be truly strong. But that strength is illusory, for it is fashioned within the context of male models of power.

As women, we have come to distrust that power which rises from our deepest and nonrational knowledge. We have been warned against it all our lives by the male world, which values this depth of feeling enough to keep women around in order to exercise it in the service of men, but which fears this same depth too much to examine the possibilities of it within themselves. So women are maintained at a distant/inferior position to be psychically milked, much the same way ants maintain colonies of aphids to provide a lifegiving substance for their masters.

But the erotic offers a well of replenishing and provocative force to the woman who does not fear its revelation, nor succumb to the belief that sensation is enough.

The erotic has often been misnamed by men and used against women. It has been made into the confused, the trivial, the psychotic, the plasticized sensation. For this reason, we have often turned away from the exploration and consideration of the erotic as a source of power and information, confusing it with its opposite, the pornographic. But pornography is a direct denial of the power of the erotic, for it represents the suppression of true feeling. Pornography emphasizes sensation without feeling.

The erotic is a measure between the beginnings of our sense of self and the chaos of our strongest feelings. It is an internal sense of satisfaction to which, once we have experienced it, we know we can aspire. For having experienced the fullness of this depth of feeling and recognizing its power, in honor and self-respect we can require no less of ourselves.

It is never easy to demand the most from ourselves, from our lives, from our work. To encourage excellence is to go beyond the encouraged mediocrity of our society is to encourage excellence. But giving in to the fear of feeling and working to capacity is a luxury only the unintentional can afford, and the unintentional are those who do not wish to guide their own destinies.

This internal requirement toward excellence which we learn from the erotic must not be misconstrued as demanding the impossible from ourselves nor from others. Such a demand incapacitates everyone in the process. For the erotic is not a question only of what we do; it is a question of how acutely and fully we can feel in the doing. Once we know the extent to which we are capable of feeling that sense of satisfaction and completion, we can then observe which of our various life endeavors bring us closest to that fullness.

The aim of each thing which we do is to make our lives and the lives of our children richer and more possible. Within the celebration of the erotic in all our endeavors, my work becomes a conscious decision—a longed-for bed which I enter gratefully and from which I rise up empowered.

Of course, women so empowered are dangerous. So we are taught to separate the erotic demand from most vital areas of our lives other than sex. And the lack of concern for the erotic root and satisfactions of our work is felt in our disaffection from so much of what we do. For instance, how often do we truly love our work even at its most difficult?

The principal horror of any system which defines the good in terms of profit rather than in terms of human need, or which defines human need to the exclusion of the psychic and emotional components of that need—the principal horror of such a system is that it robs our work of its erotic value, its erotic power and life appeal and fulfillment. Such a system reduces work to a travesty of necessities, a duty by which we earn bread or oblivion for ourselves and those we love. But this is tantamount to blinding a painter and then telling her to improve her work, and to enjoy the act of painting. It is not only next to impossible, it is also profoundly cruel.

As women, we need to examine the ways in which our world can be truly different. I am speaking here of the necessity for reassessing the quality of all the aspects of our lives and of our work, and of how we move toward and through them. The very word *erotic* comes from the Greek word *eros*, the personification of love in all its aspects—born of Chaos, and personifying creative power and harmony. When I speak of the erotic, then, I speak of it as an assertion of the lifeforce of women; of that creative energy empowered, the knowledge and use of which we are now reclaiming in our language, our history, our dancing, our loving, our work, our lives.

There are frequent attempts to equate pornography and eroticism, two diametrically opposed uses of the sexual. Because of these attempts, it has become fashionable to separate the spiritual (psychic and emotional) from the political, to see them as contradictory or antithetical. "What do you mean, a poetic revolutionary, a meditating gunrunner?" In the same way, we have attempted to separate the spiritual and the erotic, thereby reducing the spiritual to a world of flattened affect, a world of the ascetic who aspires to feel nothing. But nothing is farther from the truth. For the ascetic position is one of the highest fear, the gravest immobility. The severe abstinence of the ascetic becomes the ruling obsession. And it is one not of self-discipline but of self-abnegation.

The dichotomy between the spiritual and the political is also false, resulting from an incomplete attention to our erotic knowledge. For the bridge which connects them is formed by the erotic—the sensual—those physical, emotional, and psychic expressions of what is deepest and strongest and richest within each of us, being shared: the passions of love, in its deepest meanings.

Beyond the superficial, the considered phrase, "It feels right to me," acknowledges the strength of the erotic into a true knowledge, for what that means is the first and most powerful guiding light toward any understanding. And understanding is a hand-maiden which can only wait upon, or clarify, that knowledge, deeply born. The erotic is the nurturer or nursemaid of all our deepest knowledge.

The erotic functions for me in several ways, and the first is in providing the power which comes from sharing deeply any pursuit with another person. The sharing of joy, whether physical, emotional, psychic, or intellectual, forms a bridge between the sharers which can be the basis for understanding much of what is not shared between them, and lessens the threat of their difference.

Another important way in which the erotic connection functions is the open and fearless underlining of my capacity for joy. In the way my body stretches to music and opens into response, hearkening to its deepest rhythms, so every level upon which I sense also opens to the erotically satisfying experience, whether it is dancing, building a bookcase, writing a poem, examining an idea.

That self-connection shared is a measure of the joy which I know myself to be capable of feeling, a reminder of my capacity for feeling. And that deep and irreplaceable knowledge of my capacity for joy comes to demand from all of my life that it be lived within the knowledge that such satisfaction is possible, and does not have to be called *marriage*, nor *god*, nor *an afterlife*.

This is one reason why the erotic is so feared, and so often relegated to the bedroom alone, when it is recognized at all. For once we begin to feel deeply all the aspects of our lives, we begin to demand from ourselves and from our life-pursuits that they feel in accordance with that joy which we know ourselves to be capable of. Our erotic knowledge empowers us, becomes a lens through which we scrutinize all aspects of our existence, forcing us to evaluate those aspects honestly in terms of their relative meaning within our lives. And this is a grave responsibility, projected from within each of us, not to settle for the convenient, the shoddy, the conventionally expected, nor the merely safe.

During World War II, we bought sealed plastic packets of white, uncolored margarine, with a tiny, intense pellet of yellow coloring perched like a topaz just inside the clear skin of the bag. We would leave the margarine out for a while to soften, and then we would pinch the little pellet to break it inside the bag, releasing the rich yellowness into the soft pale mass of margarine. Then taking it carefully between our fingers, we would knead it gently back and forth, over and over, until the color had spread throughout the whole pound bag of margarine, thoroughly coloring it.

I find the erotic such a kernel within myself. When released from its intense and constrained pellet, it flows through and colors my life with a kind of energy that heightens and sensitizes and strengthens all my experience.

We have been raised to fear the yes within ourselves, our deepest cravings. But, once recognized, those which do not enhance our future lose their power and can be altered. The fear of our desires keeps them suspect and indiscriminately powerful, for to suppress any truth is to give it strength beyond endurance. The fear that we cannot grow beyond whatever distortions we may find within ourselves keeps us docile and loyal and obedient, externally defined, and leads us to accept many facets of our oppression as women.

When we live outside ourselves, and by that I mean on external directives only rather than from our internal knowledge and needs, when we live away from those erotic guides from within ourselves, then our lives are limited by external and alien forms, and we conform to the needs of a structure that is not based on human need, let alone an individual's. But when we begin to live from within outward, in touch with the power of the erotic within ourselves, and allowing that power to inform and illuminate our actions upon the world around us, then we begin to be responsible to ourselves in the deepest sense. For as we begin to recognize our deepest feelings, we begin to give up, of necessity, being satisfied with suffering and self-negation, and with the numbness which so often seems like their only alternative in our society. Our acts against oppression become integral with self, motivated and empowered from within.

In touch with the erotic, I become less willing to accept powerlessness, or those other supplied states of being which are not native to me, such as resignation, despair, self-effacement, depression, self-denial.

And yes, there is a hierarchy. There is a difference between painting a back fence and writing a poem, but only one of quantity. And there is, for me, no difference between writing a good poem and moving into sunlight against the body of a woman I love.

This brings me to the last consideration of the erotic. To share the power of each other's feelings is different from using another's feelings as we would use a kleenex. When we look the other way from our experience, erotic or otherwise, we use rather than share the feelings of those others who participate in the experience with us. And use without consent of the used is abuse.

In order to be utilized, our erotic feelings must be recognized. The need for sharing deep feeling is a human need. But within the european-american tradition, this need is satisfied by certain proscribed erotic comings-together. These occasions are almost always characterized by a simultaneous looking away, a pretense of calling them something else, whether a religion, a fit, mob violence, or even playing doctor. And this misnaming of the need and the deed give rise to that distortion which results in pornography and obscenity—the abuse of feeling.

When we look away from the importance of the erotic in the development and sustenance of our power, or when we look away from ourselves as we satisfy our erotic needs in concert with others, we use each other as objects of satisfaction rather than share our joy in the satisfying, rather than make connection with our similarities and our differences. To refuse to be conscious of what we are feeling at any time, however comfortable that might seem, is to deny a large part of the experience, and to allow ourselves to be reduced to the pornographic, the abused, and the absurd.

The erotic cannot be felt secondhand. As a Black lesbian feminist, I have a particular feeling, knowledge, and understanding for those sisters with whom I have danced hard, played, or even fought. This deep participation has often been the forerunner for joint concerted actions not possible before.

But this erotic charge is not easily shared by women who continue to operate under an exclusively european-american male tradition. I know it was not available to me when I was trying to adapt my consciousness to this mode of living and sensation.

Only now, I find more and more women-identified women brave enough to risk sharing the erotic's electrical charge without having to look away, and without distorting the enormously powerful and creative nature of that exchange. Recognizing the power of the erotic within our lives can give us the energy to pursue genuine change within our world, rather than merely settling for a shift of characters in the same weary drama.

For not only do we touch our most profoundly creative source, but we do that which is female and self-affirming in the face of a racist, patriarchal, and anti-erotic society.

The Master's Tools
Will Never Dismantle
the Master's House

I agreed to take part in a New York University Institute for the Humanities conference a year ago, with the understanding that I would be commenting upon papers dealing with the role of difference within the lives of american women: difference of race, sexuality, class, and age. The absence of these considerations weakens any feminist discussion of the personal and the political.

It is a particular academic arrogance to assume any discussion of feminist theory without examining our many differences, and without a significant input from poor women, Black and Third World women, and lesbians. And yet, I stand here as a Black lesbian feminist, having been invited to comment within the only panel at this conference where the input of Black feminists and lesbians is represented. What this says about the vision of this conference is sad, in a country where racism, sexism, and homophobia are inseparable. To read this program is to assume that lesbian and Black women have nothing to say about existentialism, the erotic, women's culture and silence, developing feminist theory, or heterosexuality and power. And what does it mean in personal and political terms when even the two Black women who did present here were literally found at the last hour? What does it mean when the tools of a racist patriarchy are used to examine the fruits of that same patriarchy? It means that only the most narrow perimeters of change are possible and allowable.

The absence of any consideration of lesbian consciousness or the consciousness of Third World women leaves a serious gap within this conference and within the papers presented here. For example, in a paper on material relationships between women, I was conscious of an either/or model of nurturing which totally dismissed my knowledge as a Black lesbian. In this paper there was no examination of mutuality between women, no systems of shared support, no interdependence as exists between lesbians and women-identified women. Yet it is only in the patriarchal model of nurturance that women "who attempt to emancipate themselves pay perhaps too high a price for the results," as this paper states.

For women, the need and desire to nurture each other is not pathological but redemptive, and it is within that knowledge that our real power is rediscovered. It is this real connection which is so feared by a patriarchal world. Only within a patriarchal structure is maternity the only social power open to women.

Interdependency between women is the way to a freedom which allows the *I* to *be*, not in order to be used, but in order to be creative. This is a difference between the passive *be* and the active *being*.

Advocating the mere tolerance of difference between women is the grossest reformism. It is a total denial of the creative function of difference in our lives. Difference must be not merely tolerated, but seen as a fund of necessary polarities between which our creativity can spark like a dialectic. Only then does the necessity for interdependency become unthreatening. Only within that interdependency of different strengths, acknowledged and equal, can the power to seek new ways of being in the world generate, as well as the courage and sustenance to act where there are no charters.

Within the interdependence of mutual (nondominant) differences lies that security which enables us to descend into the chaos of knowledge and return with true visions of our future, along with the concomitant power to effect those changes which can bring that future into being. Difference is that raw and powerful connection from which our personal power is forged.

As women, we have been taught either to ignore our differences, or to view them as causes for separation and suspicion rather than as forces for change. Without community there is no liberation, only the most vulnerable and temporary armistice between an individual and her oppression. But community must not mean a shedding of our differences, nor the pathetic pretense that these differences do not exist.

Those of us who stand outside the circle of this society's definition of acceptable women; those of us who have been forged in the crucibles of difference—those of us who are poor, who are lesbians, who are Black, who are older—know that *survival is not an academic skill*. It is learning how to stand alone, unpopular and sometimes reviled, and how to make common cause with those others identified as outside the structures in order to define and seek a world in which we can all flourish. It is learning how to take our differences and make them strengths. *For the master's tools will never dismantle the master's house.* They may allow us temporarily to beat him at his own game, but they will never enable us to bring about genuine change. And this fact is only threatening to those women who still define the master's house as their only source of support.

Poor women and women of Color know there is a difference between the daily manifestations of marital slavery and prostitution because it is our daughters who line 42nd Street. If white american feminist theory need not deal with the differences between us, and the resulting difference in our oppressions, then how do you deal with the fact that the women who clean your houses and tend your children while you attend conferences on feminist theory are, for the most part, poor women and women of Color? What is the theory behind racist feminism?

In a world of possibility for us all, our personal visions help lay the groundwork for political action. The failure of academic feminists to recognize difference as a crucial strength is a failure to reach beyond the first patriarchal lesson. In our world, divide and conquer must become define and empower.

Why weren't other women of Color found to participate in this conference? Why were two phone calls to me considered a consultation? Am I the only possible source of names of Black feminists? And although the Black panelist's paper ends on an important and powerful connection of love between women, what about interracial cooperation between feminists who don't love each other?

In academic feminist circles, the answer to these questions is often, "We did not know who to ask." But that is the same evasion of responsibility, the same cop-out, that keeps Black women's art out of women's exhibitions, Black women's work out of most feminist publications except for the occasional "Special Third World Women's Issue," and Black women's texts off your reading lists. But as Adrienne Rich pointed out in a recent talk, white feminists have educated themselves about such an enormous amount over the past ten years, how come you haven't also educated yourselves about Black women and the differences between us—white and Black—when it is key to our survival as a movement?

Women of today are still being called upon to stretch across the gap of male ignorance and to educate men as to our existence and our needs. This is an old and primary tool of all oppressors to keep the oppressed occupied with the master's concerns. Now we hear that it is the task of women of Color to educate white women—in the face of tremendous resistance—as to our existence, our differences, our relative roles in our joint survival. This is a diversion of energies and a tragic repetition of racist patriarchal thought.

Simone de Beauvoir once said: "It is in the knowledge of the genuine conditions of our lives that we must draw our strength to live and our reasons for acting."

Racism and homophobia are real conditions of all our lives in this place and time. *I urge each one of us here to reach down into that deep place of knowledge inside herself and touch that terror and loathing of any difference that lives there. See whose face it wears.* Then the personal as the political can begin to illuminate all our choices.

Sexism

An American Disease in Blackface

Black feminism is not white feminism in blackface. Black women have particular and legitimate issues which affect our lives as Black women, and addressing those issues does not make us any less Black. To attempt to open dialogue between Black women and Black men by attacking Black feminists seems shortsighted and self-defeating. Yet this is what Robert Staples, Black sociologist, has done in *The Black Scholar*.

Despite our recent economic gains, Black women are still the lowest paid group in the nation by sex and race. This gives some idea of the inequity from which we started. In Staples' own words, Black women in 1979 only *"threaten* to overtake black men" [italics mine] by the "next century" in education, occupation, and income. In other words, the inequity is self-evident; but how is it justifiable?

Black feminists speak as women because we are women and do not need others to speak for us. It is for Black men to speak up and tell us why and how their manhood is so threatened that Black women should be the prime targets of their justifiable rage. What correct analysis of this capitalist dragon within which we live can legitimize the rape of Black women by Black men?

At least Black feminists and other Black women have begun this much-needed dialogue, however bitter our words. At least we are not mowing down our brothers in the street, or bludgeoning them to death with hammers. Yet. We recognize the fallacies of separatist solutions.

Staples pleads his cause by saying capitalism has left the Black man only his penis for fulfillment, and a "curious rage." Is this rage any more legitimate than the rage of Black women? And why are Black women supposed to absorb that male rage in silence? Why isn't that male rage turned upon those forces which limit his fulfillment, namely capitalism? Staples sees in Ntozake Shange's play *For Colored Girls* "a collective appetite for black male blood." Yet it is my female children and my Black sisters who lie bleeding all around me, victims of the appetites of our brothers.

Into what theoretical analysis would Staples fit Patricia Cowan? She answered an ad in Detroit for a Black actress to audition in a play called *Hammer*. As she acted out an argument scene, watched by the playwright's brother and her four-year-old son, the Black male playwright picked up a sledgehammer and bludgeoned her to death. Will Staples' "compassion for misguided black men" bring this young mother back, or make her senseless death more acceptable?

Black men's feelings of cancellation, their grievances, and their fear of vulnerability must be talked about, but not by Black women when it is at the expense of our own "curious rage."

If this society ascribes roles to Black men which they are not allowed to fulfill, is it Black women who must bend and alter our lives to compensate, or is it society that needs changing? And why should Black men accept these roles as correct ones, or anything other than a narcotic promise encouraging acceptance of other facets of their own oppression?

One tool of the Great-American-Double-Think is to blame the victim for victimization: Black people are said to invite lynching by not knowing our place; Black women are said to invite rape and murder and abuse by not being submissive enough, or by being too seductive, or too . . .

Staples' "fact" that Black women get their sense of fulfillment from having children is only a fact when stated out of the mouths of Black men, and any Black person in this country, even a "happily married" woman who has "no pent-up frustrations that need release" (!) is either a fool or insane. This smacks of the oldest sexist canard of all time, that all a woman needs to "keep her quiet" is a "good man." File that one alongside "Some of my best friends are . . ."

Instead of beginning the much-needed dialogue between Black men and Black women, Staples retreats to a defensive stance reminiscent of white liberals of the 60s, many of whom saw any statement of Black pride and self-assertion as an automatic threat to their own identity and an attempt to wipe them out. Here we have an intelligent Black man believing—or at least saying—that any call to Black women to love ourselves (and no one said *only*) is a denial of, or threat to, his Black male identity!

In this country, Black women traditionally have had compassion for everybody else except ourselves. We have cared for whites because we had to for pay or survival; we have cared for our children and our fathers and our brothers and our lovers. History and popular culture, as well as our personal lives, are full of tales of Black women who had "compassion for misguided black men." Our scarred, broken, battered and dead daughters and sisters are a mute testament to that reality. We need to learn to have care and compassion for ourselves, also.

In the light of what Black women often willingly sacrifice for our children and our men, this is a much needed exhortation, no matter what illegitimate use the white media makes of it. This call for self-value and self-love is quite different from narcissism, as Staples must certainly realize. Narcissism comes not out of self-love but out of self-hatred.

The lack of a reasonable and articulate Black male viewpoint on these questions is not the responsibility of Black women. We have too often been expected to be all things to all people and speak everyone else's position but our very own. Black men are not so passive that they must have Black women speak for them. Even my fourteen-year-old son knows that. Black men themselves must examine and articulate their own desires and positions and stand by the conclusions thereof. No point is served by a Black male professional who merely whines at the absence of his viewpoint in Black women's work. Oppressors always expect the oppressed to extend to them the understanding so lacking in themselves.

For Staples to suggest, for instance, that Black men leave their families as a form of male protest against female decision making in the home is in direct contradiction to his own observations in "The Myth of the Black Matriarchy."[*]

Now I am sure there are still some Black men who marry white women because they feel a white woman can better fit the model of "femininity" set forth in this country. But for Staples to justify that act using the reason it occurs, and take Black women to task for it, is not only another error in reasoning; it is like justifying the actions of a lemming who follows its companions over the cliff to sure death. Because it happens does

[*] "The Myth of the Black Matriarchy" by Robert Staples in *The Black Scholar*, vol. 1, no. 3–4 (January–February 1970).

not mean it should happen, nor that it is functional for the well-being of the individual nor the group.

It is not the destiny of Black america to repeat white america's mistakes. But we will, if we mistake the trappings of success in a sick society for the signs of a meaningful life. If Black men continue to define "femininity" instead of their own desires, and to do it in archaic european terms, they restrict our access to each other's energies. Freedom and future for Blacks does not mean absorbing the dominant white male disease of sexism.

As Black women and men, we cannot hope to begin dialogue by denying the oppressive nature of male privilege. And if Black males choose to assume that privilege for whatever reason—raping, brutalizing, and killing Black women—then ignoring these acts of Black male oppression within our communities can only serve our destroyers. One oppression does not justify another.

It has been said that Black men cannot be denied their personal choice of the woman who meets their need to dominate. In that case, Black women also cannot be denied our personal choices, and those choices are becomingly increasingly self-assertive and female-oriented.

As a people, we most certainly must work together. It would be shortsighted to believe that Black men alone are to blame for the above situations in a society dominated by white male privilege. But the Black male consciousness must be raised to the realization that sexism and woman-hating are critically dysfunctional to his liberation as a Black man because they arise out of the same constellation that engenders racism and homophobia. Until that consciousness is developed, Black men will view sexism and the destruction of Black women as tangential to Black liberation rather than as central to that struggle. So long as this occurs, we will never be able to embark upon that dialogue between Black women and Black men that is so essential to our survival as a people. This continued blindness between us can only serve the oppressive system within which we live.

Men avoid women's observations by accusing us of being too "visceral." But no amount of understanding the roots of Black woman-hating will bring back Patricia Cowan, nor mute her family's loss. Pain is very visceral, particularly to the people who are hurting. As the poet Mary McAnally said, "Pain teaches us to take our fingers OUT the fucking fire."[*]

If the problems of Black women are only derivatives of a larger contradiction between capital and labor, then so is racism, and both must be fought by all of us. The capitalist structure is a many-headed monster. I might add here that in no socialist country that I have visited have I found an absence of racism or of sexism, so the eradication of both of these diseases seems to involve more than the abolition of capitalism as an institution.

No reasonable Black man can possibly condone the rape and slaughter of Black women by Black men as a fitting response to capitalist oppression. And destruction of Black women by Black men clearly cuts across all class lines.

Whatever the "structural underpinnings" (Staples) for sexism in the Black community may be, it is obviously Black women who are bearing the brunt of that sexism, and so it is in our best interest to abolish it. We invite our Black brothers to join us, since ultimately that abolition is in their best interests also. For Black men are also diminished by a sexism which robs them of meaningful connections to Black women and our struggles. Since it is Black women who are being abused,

---

[*] From *We Will Make A River*, poems by Mary McAnnally (West End Press, Cambridge, Massachusetts, 1979), p. 27.

however, and since it is our female blood that is being shed, it is for Black women to decide whether or not sexism in the Black community is pathological. And we do not approach that discussion theoretically. Those "creative relationships" which Staples speaks about within the Black community are almost invariably those which operate to the benefit of Black males, given the Black male/female ratio and the implied power balance within a supply and demand situation. Polygamy is seen as "creative," but a lesbian relationship is not. This is much the same as how the "creative relationships" between master and slave were always those benefiting the master.

The results of woman-hating in the Black community are tragedies which diminish all Black people. These acts must be seen in the context of a systematic devaluation of Black women within this society. It is within this context that we become approved and acceptable targets for Black male rage, so acceptable that even a Black male social scientist condones and excuses this depersonalizing abuse.

This abuse is no longer acceptable to Black women in the name of solidarity, nor of Black liberation. Any dialogue between Black women and Black men must begin there, no matter where it ends.

The Uses of Anger

Women Responding to Racism

*R*acism. The belief in the inherent superiority of one race over all others and thereby the right to dominance, manifest and implied.

Women respond to racism. My response to racism is anger. I have lived with that anger, ignoring it, feeding upon it, learning to use it before it laid my visions to waste, for most of my life. Once I did it in silence, afraid of the weight. My fear of anger taught me nothing. Your fear of that anger will teach you nothing, also.

Women responding to racism means women responding to anger; the anger of exclusion, of unquestioned privilege, of racial distortions, of silence, ill-use, stereotyping, defensiveness, misnaming, betrayal, and cooptation.

My anger is a response to racist attitudes and to the actions and presumptions that arise out of those attitudes. If your dealings with other women reflect those attitudes, then my anger and your attendant fears are spotlights that can be used for growth in the same way I have used learning to express anger for my growth. But for corrective surgery, not guilt. Guilt and defensiveness are bricks in a wall against which we all flounder; they serve none of our futures.

Because I do not want this to become a theoretical discussion, I am going to give a few examples of interchanges between women that illustrate these points. In the interest of time, I am going to cut them short. I want you to know there were many more.

For example:

- I speak out of direct and particular anger at an academic conference, and a white woman says, "Tell me how you feel but don't say it too harshly or I cannot hear you." But is it my manner that keeps her from hearing, or the threat of a message that her life may change?

- The Women's Studies Program of a southern university invites a Black woman to read following a week-long forum on Black and white women. "What has this week given to you?" I ask. The most vocal white woman says, "I think I've gotten a lot. I feel Black women really understand me a lot better now; they have a better idea of where I'm coming from." As if understanding her lay at the core of the racist problem.

- After fifteen years of a women's movement which professes to address the life concerns and possible futures of all women, I still hear, on campus after campus, "How can we address the issues of racism? No women of Color attended." Or, the other side of that statement, "We have no one in our department equipped to teach their work." In other words, racism is a Black women's problem, a problem of women of Color, and only we can discuss it.

- After I read from my work entitled "Poems for Women in Rage,"* a white woman asks me: "Are you going to do anything with how we can deal directly with *our* anger? I feel it's so important." I ask, "How do you use *your* rage?" And then I have to turn away from the blank look in her eyes, before she can invite me to participate in her own annihilation. I do not exist to feel her anger for her.

- White women are beginning to examine their relationships to Black women, yet often I hear them wanting only to deal with little colored children across the roads of childhood, the beloved nursemaid, the occasional second-grade classmate—those tender memories of what was once mysterious and intriguing or neutral. You avoid the childhood assumptions formed by the raucous laughter at Rastus and Alfalfa, the acute message of your mommy's handerkerchief spread upon the park bench because I had just been sitting there, the indelible and dehumanizing portraits of Amos 'n Andy and your daddy's humorous bedtime stories.

- I wheel my two-year-old daughter in a shopping cart through a supermarket in Eastchester in 1967, and a little white girl riding past in her mother's cart calls out excitedly, "Oh look, Mommy, a baby maid!" And your mother shushes you, but she does not correct you. And so fifteen years later, at a conference on racism, you can still find that story humorous. But I hear your laughter is full of terror and disease.

---

* One poem from this series is included in *Chosen Poems: Old and New* (W. W. Norton & Company, New York, 1978), pp. 105–108.

- A white academic welcomes the appearance of a collection by non-Black women of Color.* "It allows me to deal with racism without dealing with the harshness of Black women," she says to me.

- At an international cultural gathering of women, a well-known white American woman poet interrupts the reading of the work of women of Color to read her own poem, and then dashes off to an "important panel."

If women in the academy truly want a dialogue about racism, it will require recognizing the needs and the living contexts of other women. When an academic woman says, "I can't afford it," she may mean she is making a choice about how to spend her available money. But when a woman on welfare says, "I can't afford it," she means she is surviving on an amount of money that was barely subsistence in 1972, and she often does not have enough to eat. Yet the National Women's Studies Association here in 1981 holds a conference in which it commits itself to responding to racism, yet refuses to waive the registration fee for poor women and women of Color who wished to present and conduct workshops. This has made it impossible for many women of Color—for instance, Wilmette Brown, of Black Women for Wages for Housework—to participate in this conference. Is this to be merely another case of the academy discussing life within the closed circuits of the academy?

To the white women present who recognize these attitudes as familiar, but most of all, to all my sisters of Color who live and survive thousands of such encounters—to my sisters of

---

* *This Bridge Called My Back: Writings by Radical Women of Color* edited by Cherríe Moraga and Gloria Anzaldua (Kitchen Table: Women of Color Press, New York, 1984), first published in 1981.

Color who like me still tremble their rage under harness, or who sometimes question the expression of our rage as useless and disruptive (the two most popular accusations)—I want to speak about anger, my anger, and what I have learned from my travels through its dominions.

Everything can be used / except what is wasteful / (you will need / to remember this when you are accused of destruction.) *

Every woman has a well-stocked arsenal of anger potentially useful against those oppressions, personal and institutional, which brought that anger into being. Focused with precision it can become a powerful source of energy serving progress and change. And when I speak of change, I do not mean a simple switch of positions or a temporary lessening of tensions, nor the ability to smile or feel good. I am speaking of a basic and radical alteration in those assumptions underlining our lives.

I have seen situations where white women hear a racist remark, resent what has been said, become filled with fury, and remain silent because they are afraid. That unexpressed anger lies within them like an undetonated device, usually to be hurled at the first woman of Color who talks about racism.

But anger expressed and translated into action in the service of our vision and our future is a liberating and strengthening act of clarification, for it is in the painful process of this translation that we identify who are our allies with whom we have grave differences, and who are our genuine enemies.

Anger is loaded with information and energy. When I speak of women of Color, I do not only mean Black women. The woman of Color who is not Black and who charges me with

---

* From "For Each of You," first published in *From A Land Where Other People Live* (Broadside Press, Detroit, 1973), and collected in *Chosen Poems: Old and New* (W. W. Norton & Company, New York, 1982), p. 42.

rendering her invisible by assuming that her struggles with racism are identical with my own has something to tell me that I had better learn from, lest we both waste ourselves fighting the truths between us. If I participate, knowingly or otherwise, in my sister's oppression and she calls me on it, to answer her anger with my own only blankets the substance of our exchange with reaction. It wastes energy. And yes, it is very difficult to stand still and to listen to another woman's voice delineate an agony I do not share, or one to which I myself have contributed.

In this place we speak removed from the more blatant reminders of our embattlement as women. This need not blind us to the size and complexities of the forces mounting against us and all that is most human within our environment. We are not here as women examining racism in a political and social vacuum. We operate in the teeth of a system for which racism and sexism are primary, established, and necessary props of profit. Women responding to racism is a topic so dangerous that when the local media attempt to discredit this conference they choose to focus upon the provision of lesbian housing as a diversionary device—as if the Hartford *Courant* dare not mention the topic chosen for discussion here, racism, lest it become apparent that women are in fact attempting to examine and to alter all the repressive conditions of our lives.

Mainstream communication does not want women, particularly white women, responding to racism. It wants racism to be accepted as an immutable given in the fabric of your existence, like evening time or the common cold.

So we are working in a context of opposition and threat, the cause of which is certainly not the angers which lie between us, but rather that virulent hatred leveled against all women, people of Color, lesbians and gay men, poor people—against all of us who are seeking to examine the particulars of our lives as we resist our oppressions, moving toward coalition and effective action.

Any discussion among women about racism must include the recognition and the use of anger. This discussion must be direct and creative because it is crucial. We cannot allow our fear of anger to deflect us nor seduce us into settling for anything less than the hard work of excavating honesty; we must be quite serious about the choice of this topic and the angers entwined within it because, rest assured, our opponents are quite serious about their hatred of us and of what we are trying to do here.

And while we scrutinize the often painful face of each other's anger, please remember that it is not our anger which makes me caution you to lock your doors at night and not to wander the streets of Hartford alone. It is the hatred which lurks in those streets, that urge to destroy us all if we truly work for change rather than merely indulge in academic rhetoric.

This hatred and our anger are very different. Hatred is the fury of those who do not share our goals, and its object is death and destruction. Anger is a grief of distortions between peers, and its object is change. But our time is getting shorter. We have been raised to view any difference other than sex as a reason for destruction, and for Black women and white women to face each other's angers without denial or immobility or silence or guilt is in itself a heretical and generative idea. It implies peers meeting upon a common basis to examine difference, and to alter those distortions which history has created around our difference. For it is those distortions which separate us. And we must ask ourselves: Who profits from all this?

Women of Color in america have grown up within a symphony of anger, at being silenced, at being unchosen, at knowing that when we survive, it is in spite of a world that takes for granted our lack of humanness, and which hates our very existence outside of its service. And I say *symphony* rather than *cacophony* because we have had to learn to orchestrate those furies so that they do not tear us apart. We have had to learn to move through them and use them for strength and force and insight within our daily lives. Those of us who did not learn this difficult lesson did not survive. And part of my anger is always libation for my fallen sisters.

Anger is an appropriate reaction to racist attitudes, as is fury when the actions arising from those attitudes do not change. To those women here who fear the anger of women of Color more than their own unscrutinized racist attitudes, I ask: Is the anger of women of Color more threatening than the woman-hatred that tinges all aspects of our lives?

It is not the anger of other women that will destroy us but our refusals to stand still, to listen to its rhythms, to learn within it, to move beyond the manner of presentation to the substance, to tap that anger as an important source of empowerment.

I cannot hide my anger to spare you guilt, nor hurt feelings, nor answering anger; for to do so insults and trivializes all our efforts. Guilt is not a response to anger; it is a response to one's own actions or lack of action. If it leads to change then it can be useful, since it is then no longer guilt but the beginning of knowledge. Yet all too often, guilt is just another name for impotence, for defensiveness destructive of communication; it becomes a device to protect ignorance and the continuation of things the way they are, the ultimate protection for changelessness.

Most women have not developed tools for facing anger constructively. CR groups in the past, largely white, dealt with how to express anger, usually at the world of men. And these groups were made up of white women who shared the terms of their oppressions. There was usually little attempt to articulate the genuine differences between women, such as those of race, color, age, class, and sexual identity. There was no apparent need at that time to examine the contradictions of self, woman as oppressor. There was work on expressing anger, but very little on anger directed against each other. No tools were developed to deal with other women's anger except to avoid it, deflect it, or flee from it under a blanket of guilt.

I have no creative use for guilt, yours or my own. Guilt is only another way of avoiding informed action, of buying time out of the pressing need to make clear choices, out of the approaching storm that can feed the earth as well as bend the trees. If I speak to you in anger, at least I have spoken to you: I have not put a gun to your head and shot you down in the street; I have not looked at your bleeding sister's body and asked, "What did she do to deserve it?" This was the reaction of two white women to Mary Church Terrell's telling of the lynching of a pregnant Black woman whose baby was then torn from her body. That was in 1921, and Alice Paul had just refused to publicly endorse the enforcement of the Nineteenth Amendment for all women—by refusing to endorse the inclusion of women of Color, although we had worked to help bring about that amendment.

The angers between women will not kill us if we can articulate them with precision, if we listen to the content of what is said with at least as much intensity as we defend ourselves against the manner of saying. When we turn from anger we turn from insight, saying we will accept only the designs already known, deadly and safely familiar. I have tried to learn my anger's usefulness to me, as well as its limitations.

For women raised to fear, too often anger threatens annihilation. In the male construct of brute force, we were taught that our lives depended upon the good will of patriarchal power. The anger of others was to be avoided at all costs because there was nothing to be learned from it but pain, a judgment that we had been bad girls, come up lacking, not done what we were supposed to do. And if we accept our powerlessness, then of course any anger can destroy us.

But the strength of women lies in recognizing differences between us as creative, and in standing to those distortions which we inherited without blame, but which are now ours to alter. The angers of women can transform difference through insight into power. For anger between peers births change, not destruction, and the discomfort and sense of loss it often causes is not fatal, but a sign of growth.

My response to racism is anger. That anger has eaten clefts into my living only when it remained unspoken, useless to anyone. It has also served me in classrooms without light or learning, where the work and history of Black women was less than a vapor. It has served me as fire in the ice zone of uncomprehending eyes of white women who see in my experience and the experience of my people only new reasons for fear or guilt. And my anger is no excuse for not dealing with your blindness, no reason to withdraw from the results of your own actions.

When women of Color speak out of the anger that laces so many of our contacts with white women, we are often told that we are "creating a mood of hopelessness," "preventing white women from getting past guilt," or "standing in the way of trusting communication and action." All these quotes come directly from letters to me from members of this organization within the last two years. One woman wrote, "Because you are Black and Lesbian, you seem to speak with the moral authority of suffering." Yes, I am Black and Lesbian, and what you hear in my voice is fury, not suffering. Anger, not moral authority. There is a difference.

To turn aside from the anger of Black women with excuses

or the pretexts of intimidation is to award no one power—it is merely another way of preserving racial blindness, the power of unaddressed privilege, unbreached, intact. Guilt is only another form of objectification. Oppressed peoples are always being asked to stretch a little more, to bridge the gap between blindness and humanity. Black women are expected to use our anger only in the service of other people's salvation or learning. But that time is over. My anger has meant pain to me but it has also meant survival, and before I give it up I'm going to be sure that there is something at least as powerful to replace it on the road to clarity.

What woman here is so enamoured of her own oppression that she cannot see her heelprint upon another woman's face? What woman's terms of oppression have become precious and necessary to her as a ticket into the fold of the righteous, away from the cold winds of self-scrutiny?

I am a lesbian woman of Color whose children eat regularly because I work in a university. If their full bellies make me fail to recognize my commonality with a woman of Color whose children do not eat because she cannot find work, or who has no children because her insides are rotted from home abortions and sterilization; if I fail to recognize the lesbian who chooses not to have children, the woman who remains closeted because her homophobic community is her only life support, the woman who chooses silence instead of another death, the woman who is terrified lest my anger trigger the explosion of hers; if I fail to recognize them as other faces of myself, then I am contributing not only to each of their oppressions but also to my own, and the anger which stands between us then must be used for clarity and mutual empowerment, not for evasion by guilt or for further separation. I am not free while any woman is unfree, even when her shackles are very different from my own. And I am not free as long as one person of Color remains chained. Nor is any one of you.

I speak here as a woman of Color who is not bent upon destruction, but upon survival. No woman is responsible for altering the psyche of her oppressor, even when that psyche is embodied in another woman. I have suckled the wolf's lip of anger and I have used it for illumination, laughter, protection, fire in places where there was no light, no food, no sisters, no quarter. We are not goddesses or matriarchs or edifices of divine forgiveness; we are not fiery fingers of judgment or instruments of flagellation; we are women forced back always upon our woman's power. We have learned to use anger as we have learned to use the dead flesh of animals, and bruised, battered, and changing, we have survived and grown and, in Angela Wilson's words, we *are* moving on. With or without uncolored women. We use whatever strengths we have fought for, including anger, to help define and fashion a world where all our sisters can grow, where our children can love, and where the power of touching and meeting another woman's difference and wonder will eventually transcend the need for destruction.

For it is not the anger of Black women which is dripping down over this globe like a diseased liquid. It is not my anger that launches rockets, spends over sixty thousand dollars a second on missiles and other agents of war and death, slaughters children in cities, stockpiles nerve gas and chemical bombs, sodomizes our daughters and our earth. It is not the anger of Black women which corrodes into blind, dehumanizing power, bent upon the annihilation of us all unless we meet it with what we have, our power to examine and to redefine the terms upon which we will live and work; our power to envision and to reconstruct, anger by painful anger, stone upon heavy stone, a future of pollinating difference and the earth to support our choices.

We welcome all women who can meet us, face to face, beyond objectification and beyond guilt.

Fourth of July

The first time I went to Washington, D.C. was on the edge of the summer when I was supposed to stop being a child. At least that's what they said to us all at graduation from the eighth grade. My sister Phyllis graduated at the same time from high school. I don't know what she was supposed to stop being. But as graduation presents for us both, the whole family took a Fourth of July trip to Washington, D.C., the fabled and famous capital of our country.

It was the first time I'd ever been on a railroad train during the day. When I was little, and we used to go to the Connecticut shore, we always went at night on the milk train, because it was cheaper.

Preparations were in the air around our house before school was even over. We packed for a week. There were two very large suitcases that my father carried, and a box filled with food. In fact, my first trip to Washington was a mobile feast; I started eating as soon as we were comfortably ensconced in our seats, and did not stop until somewhere after Philadelphia. I remember it was Philadelphia because I was disappointed not to have passed by the Liberty Bell.

My mother had roasted two chickens and cut them up into

dainty bite-size pieces. She packed slices of brown bread and butter and green pepper and carrot sticks. There were little violently yellow iced cakes with scalloped edges called "marigolds," that came from Cushman's Bakery. There was a spice bun and rock-cakes from Newton's, the West Indian bakery across Lenox Avenue from St. Mark's School, and iced tea in a wrapped mayonnaise jar. There were sweet pickles for us and dill pickles for my father, and peaches with the fuzz still on them, individually wrapped to keep them from bruising. And, for neatness, there were piles of napkins and a little tin box with a washcloth dampened with rosewater and glycerine for wiping sticky mouths.

I wanted to eat in the dining car because I had read all about them, but my mother reminded me for the umpteenth time that dining car food always cost too much money and besides, you never could tell whose hands had been playing all over that food, nor where those same hands had been just before. My mother never mentioned that Black people were not allowed into railroad dining cars headed south in 1947. As usual, whatever my mother did not like and could not change, she ignored. Perhaps it would go away, deprived of her attention.

I learned later that Phyllis's high school senior class trip had been to Washington, but the nuns had given her back her deposit in private, explaining to her that the class, all of whom were white, except Phyllis, would be staying in a hotel where Phyllis "would not be happy," meaning, Daddy explained to her, also in private, that they did not rent rooms to Negroes. "We will take among-you to Washington, ourselves," my father had avowed, "and not just for an overnight in some measly fleabag hotel."

American racism was a new and crushing reality that my parents had to deal with every day of their lives once they came to this country. They handled it as a private woe. My mother and father believed that they could best protect their children from the realities of race in america and the fact of american racism by never giving them name, much less discussing their nature. We were told we must never trust white people, but *why* was never explained, nor the nature of their ill will. Like so many other vital pieces of information in my childhood, I was supposed to know without being told. It always seemed like a very strange injunction coming from my mother, who looked so much like one of those people we were never supposed to trust. But something always warned me not to ask my mother why she wasn't white, and why Auntie Lillah and Auntie Etta weren't, even though they were all that same problematic color so different from my father and me, even from my sisters, who were somewhere in-between.

In Washington, D.C. we had one large room with two double beds and an extra cot for me. It was a back-street hotel that belonged to a friend of my father's who was in real estate, and I spent the whole next day after Mass squinting up at the Lincoln Memorial where Marian Anderson had sung after the D.A.R. refused to allow her to sing in their auditorium because she was Black. Or because she was "Colored," my father said as he told us the story. Except that what he probably said was "Negro," because for his times, my father was quite progressive.

I was squinting because I was in that silent agony that characterized all of my childhood summers, from the time school let out in June to the end of July, brought about by my dilated and vulnerable eyes exposed to the summer brightness.

I viewed Julys through an agonizing corolla of dazzling whiteness and I always hated the Fourth of July, even before I came to realize the travesty such a celebration was for Black people in this country.

My parents did not approve of sunglasses, nor of their expense.

I spent the afternoon squinting up at monuments to freedom and past presidencies and democracy, and wondering why the light and heat were both so much stronger in Washington, D.C. than back home in New York City. Even the pavement on the streets was a shade lighter in color than back home.

Late that Washington afternoon my family and I walked back down Pennsylvania Avenue. We were a proper caravan, mother bright and father brown, the three of us girls step-standards in between. Moved by our historical surroundings and the heat of the early evening, my father decreed yet another treat. He had a great sense of history, a flair for the quietly dramatic and the sense of specialness of an occasion and a trip.

"Shall we stop and have a little something to cool off, Lin?"

Two blocks away from our hotel, the family stopped for a dish of vanilla ice cream at a Breyer's ice cream and soda fountain. Indoors, the soda fountain was dim and fan-cooled, deliciously relieving to my scorched eyes.

Corded and crisp and pinafored, the five of us seated ourselves one by one at the counter. There was I between my mother and father, and my two sisters on the other side of my mother. We settled ourselves along the white mottled marble counter, and when the waitress spoke at first no one understood what she was saying, and so the five of us just sat there.

The waitress moved along the line of us closer to my father and spoke again. "I said I kin give you to take out, but you can't eat here. Sorry." Then she dropped her eyes looking very embarrassed, and suddenly we heard what it was she was saying all at the same time, loud and clear.

Straight-backed and indignant, one by one, my family and I got down from the counter stools and turned around and marched out of the store, quiet and outraged, as if we had never been Black before. No one would answer my emphatic questions with anything other than a guilty silence. "But we hadn't done anything!" This wasn't right or fair! Hadn't I written poems about Bataan and freedom and democracy for all?

My parents wouldn't speak of this injustice, not because they had contributed to it, but because they felt they should have anticipated it and avoided it. This made me even angrier. My fury was not going to be acknowledged by a like fury. Even my two sisters copied my parents' pretense that nothing unusual and anti-american had occurred. I was left to write my angry letter to the president of the united states all by myself, although my father did promise I could type it out on the office typewriter next week, after I showed it to him in my copybook diary.

The waitress was white, and the counter was white, and the ice cream I never ate in Washington, D.C. that summer I left childhood was white, and the white heat and the white pavement and the white stone monuments of my first Washington summer made me sick to my stomach for the whole rest of that trip and it wasn't much of a graduation present after all.

I Am Your Sister

Black Women Organizing Across Sexualities

Whenever I come to Medgar Evers College I always feel a thrill of anticipation and delight because it feels like coming home, like talking to family, having a chance to speak about things that are very important to me with people who matter the most. And this is particularly true whenever I talk at the Women's Center. But, as with all families, we sometimes find it difficult to deal constructively with the genuine differences between us and to recognize that unity does not require that we be identical to each other. Black women are not one great vat of homogenized chocolate milk. We have many different faces, and we do not have to become each other in order to work together.

It is not easy for me to speak here with you as a Black Lesbian feminist, recognizing that some of the ways in which I identify myself make it difficult for you to hear me. But meeting across difference always requires mutual stretching, and until you can hear me as a Black Lesbian feminist, our strengths will not be truly available to each other as Black women.

Because I feel it is urgent that we not waste each other's

resources, that we recognize each sister on her own terms so that we may better work together toward our mutual survival, I speak here about heterosexism and homophobia, two grave barriers to organizing among Black women. And so that we have a common language between us, I would like to define some of the terms I use:

Heterosexism—a belief in the inherent superiority of one form of loving over all others and thereby the right to dominance.

Homophobia—a terror surrounding feelings of love for members of the same sex and thereby a hatred of those feelings in others.

In the 1960s, when liberal white people decided that they didn't want to appear racist, they wore dashikis, and danced Black, and ate Black, and even married Black, but they did not want to feel Black or think Black, so they never even questioned the textures of their daily living (why should "flesh-colored" Bandaids always be pink?) and then they wondered, "Why are those Black folks always taking offense so easily at the least little thing? Some of our best friends are Black . . ."

Well, it is not necessary for some of your best friends to be Lesbian, although some of them probably are, no doubt. But it is necessary for you to stop oppressing me through false judgment. I do not want you to ignore my identity, nor do I want you to make it an insurmountable barrier between our sharing of strengths.

When I say I am a Black feminist, I mean I recognize that my power as well as my primary oppressions come as a result of my Blackness as well as my womanness, and therefore my struggles on both these fronts are inseparable.

When I say I am a Black Lesbian, I mean I am a woman

whose primary focus of loving, physical as well as emotional, is directed to women. It does not mean I hate men. Far from it. The harshest attacks I have ever heard against Black men come from those women who are intimately bound to them and cannot free themselves from a subservient and silent position. I would never presume to speak about Black men the way I have heard some of my straight sisters talk about the men they are attached to. And of course that concerns me, because it reflects a situation of noncommunication in the heterosexual Black community that is far more truly threatening than the existence of Black Lesbians.

What does this have to do with Black women organizing?

I have heard it said—usually behind my back—that Black Lesbians are not normal. But what is normal in this deranged society by which we are all trapped? I remember, and so do many of you, when being Black was considered not normal, when they talked about us in whispers, tried to paint us, lynch us, bleach us, ignore us, pretend we did not exist. We called that racism.

I have heard it said that Black Lesbians are a threat to the Black family. But when 50 percent of children born to Black women are born out of wedlock, and 30 percent of all Black families are headed by women without husbands, we need to broaden and redefine what we mean by *family*.

I have heard it said that Black Lesbians will mean the death of the race. Yet Black Lesbians bear children in exactly the same way other women bear children, and a Lesbian household is simply another kind of family. Ask my son and daughter.

The terror of Black Lesbians is buried in that deep inner place where we have been taught to fear all difference—to kill it or ignore it. Be assured: loving women is not a communicable disease. You don't catch it like the common cold. Yet the one accusation that seems to render even the most vocal straight

Black woman totally silent and ineffective is the suggestion that she might be a Black Lesbian.

If someone says you're Russian and you know you're not, you don't collapse into stunned silence. Even if someone calls you a bigamist, or a childbeater, and you know you're not, you don't crumple into bits. You say it's not true and keep on printing the posters. But let anyone, particularly a Black man, accuse a straight Black woman of being a Black *Lesbian*, and right away that sister becomes immobilized, as if that is the most horrible thing she could be, and must at all costs be proven false. That is homophobia. It is a waste of woman energy, and it puts a terrible weapon into the hands of your enemies to be used against you to silence you, to keep you docile and in line. It also serves to keep us isolated and apart.

I have heard it said that Black Lesbians are not political, that we have not been and are not involved in the struggles of Black people. But when I taught Black and Puerto Rican students writing at City College in the SEEK program in the sixties I was a Black Lesbian. I was a Black Lesbian when I helped organize and fight for the Black Studies Department of John Jay College. And because I was fifteen years younger then and less sure of myself, at one crucial moment I yielded to pressures that said I should step back for a Black man even though I knew him to be a serious error of choice, and I did, and he was. But I was a Black Lesbian then.

When my girlfriends and I went out in the car one July 4 night after fireworks with cans of white spray paint and our kids asleep in the back seat, one of us staying behind to keep the motor running and watch the kids while the other two worked our way down the suburban New Jersey street, spraying white paint over the black jockey statues, and their little red jackets, too, we were Black Lesbians.

When I drove through the Mississippi delta to Jackson in 1968 with a group of Black students from Tougaloo, another car full of redneck kids trying to bump us off the road all the way back into town, I was a Black Lesbian.

When I weaned my daughter in 1963 to go to Washington in August to work in the coffee tents along with Lena Horne, making coffee for the marshals because that was what most Black women did in the 1963 March on Washington, I was a Black Lesbian.

When I taught a poetry workshop at Tougaloo, a small Black college in Mississippi, where white rowdies shot up the edge of campus every night, and I felt the joy of seeing young Black poets find their voices and power through words in our mutual growth, I was a Black Lesbian. And there are strong Black poets today who date their growth and awareness from those workshops.

When Yoli [Yolanda Rios] and I cooked curried chicken and beans and rice and took our extra blankets and pillows up the hill to the striking students occupying buildings at City College in 1969, demanding open admissions and the right to an education, I was a Black Lesbian. When I walked through the midnight hallways of Lehman College that same year, carrying Midol and Kotex pads for the young Black radical women taking part in the action, and we tried to persuade them that their place in the revolution was not ten paces behind Black men, that spreading their legs to the guys on the tables in the cafeteria was not a revolutionary act no matter what the brothers said, I was a Black Lesbian. When I picketed for welfare mothers' rights, and against the enforced sterilization of young Black girls, when I fought institutionalized racism in the New York City schools, I was a Black Lesbian.

But you did not know it because we did not identify ourselves, so now you can say that Black Lesbians and Gay men have nothing to do with the struggles of the Black Nation.

And I am not alone.

When you read the words of Langston Hughes you are reading the words of a Black Gay man. When you read the words of Alice Dunbar-Nelson and Angelina Weld Grimké, poets of the Harlem Renaissance, you are reading the words of Black Lesbians. When you listen to the life-affirming voices of Bessie Smith and Ma Rainey, you are hearing Black Lesbian women. When you see the plays and read the words of Lorraine Hansberry, you are reading the words of a woman who loved women deeply.

Today, Lesbians and Gay men are some of the most active and engaged members of Art Against Apartheid, a group which is making visible and immediate our cultural responsibilities against the tragedy of South Africa. We have organizations such as the National Coalition of Black Lesbians and Gays, Dykes Against Racism Everywhere, and Men of All Colors Together, all of which are committed to and engaged in antiracist activity.

Homophobia and heterosexism mean you allow yourselves to be robbed of the sisterhood and strength of Black Lesbian women because you are afraid of being called a Lesbian yourself. Yet we share so many concerns as Black women, so much work to be done. The urgency of the destruction of our Black children and the theft of young Black minds are joint urgencies. Black children shot down or doped up on the streets of our cities are priorities for all of us. The fact of Black women's blood flowing with grim regularity in the streets and living rooms of Black communities is not a Black Lesbian rumor. It is sad statistical truth. The fact that there is widening and dangerous lack of communication around our differences between Black women and men is not a Black Lesbian plot. It is a reality that is starkly clarified as we see our young people becoming more and more uncaring of each other. Young Black boys believing that they can define their manhood between a sixth-grade girl's legs, growing up believing that Black women and girls are the fitting target for their justifiable furies rather than the racist structures grinding us all into dust, these are not Black Lesbian myths. These are sad realities of Black communities today and of immediate concern to us all. We cannot afford to waste each other's energies in our common battles.

What does homophobia mean? It means that high-powered Black women are told it is not safe to attend a Conference on the Status of Women in Nairobi simply because we are Lesbians. It means that in a political action, you rob yourselves of the vital insight and energies of political women such as Betty Powell and Barbara Smith and Gwendolyn Rogers and Raymina Mays and Robin Christian and Yvonne Flowers. It means another instance of the divide-and-conquer routine.

How do we organize around our differences, neither denying them nor blowing them up out of proportion?

The first step is an effort of will on your part. Try to remember to keep certain facts in mind. Black Lesbians are not apolitical. We have been a part of every freedom struggle within this country. Black Lesbians are not a threat to the Black family. Many of us have families of our own. We are not white, and we are not a disease. We are women who love women. This does not mean we are going to assault your daughters in an alley on Nostrand Avenue. It does not mean we are about to attack you if we pay you a compliment on your dress. It does not mean we only think about sex, any more than you only think about sex.

Even if you *do* believe any of these stereotypes about Black Lesbians, begin to practice *acting* like you don't believe them. Just as racist stereotypes are the problem of the white people who believe them, so also are homophobic stereotypes the problem of the heterosexuals who believe them. In other words, those stereotypes are yours to solve, not mine, and they are a terrible and wasteful barrier to our working together. I am not your enemy. We do not have to become each other's unique experiences and insights in order to share what we have learned through our particular battles for survival as Black women. . . .

There was a poster in the 1960s that was very popular: HE'S NOT BLACK, HE'S MY BROTHER! It used to infuriate me because it implied that the two were mutually exclusive—*he* couldn't be both brother and Black. Well, I do not want to be tolerated, nor misnamed. I want to be recognized.

I am a Black Lesbian, and I *am* your sister.

A Burst of Light

Living with Cancer

though we may land here there is no other landing
to choose our meaning we must make it new.

—MURIEL RUKEYSER

INTRODUCTION

The year I became fifty felt like a great coming together for me.
I was very proud of having made it for half a century, and in my
own style. "Time for a change," I thought, "I wonder how I'm
going to live the next half."

On February 1, two weeks before my fiftieth birthday, I was
told by my doctor that I had liver cancer, metastasized from the
breast cancer for which I had had a mastectomy six years before.

At first I did not believe it. I continued with my previously
planned teaching trip to europe. As I grew steadily sicker in
Berlin, I received medical information about homeopathic alter-
natives to surgery, which strengthened my decision to maintain
some control over my life for as long as possible. I believe that
decision has prolonged my life, together with the loving energies
of women who supported me in that decision and in the work
which gives that life shape.

The struggle with cancer now informs all my days, but it is only another face of that continuing battle for self-determination and survival that Black women fight daily, often in triumph. The following excerpts are from journals kept during my first three years of living with cancer.

January 15, 1984
New York City
I've just returned from three days in Washington, D.C. It was an extraordinary reading. The second evening spent with the Sapphire Sapphos was like *2001 Space Odyssey* time—the past dreaming the future blooming real and tasty into the present, now. During our evening together, I felt the love and admiration of other Black women in a way I had not before—a web woven between us of the uses to which my work has been put.

The Sapphire Sapphos are a group of Lesbians of Color who had invited me to a special dinner at their regular monthly meeting. It was held at the Clubhouse, a cozy wooden building at the back of a city lot.

Coming in out of the D.C. winter storm felt like walking into an embrace.

The roaring fireplace, the low-beamed wooden room filled with beautiful Black and Brown women, a table laden with delicious foods so obviously cooked with love. There was sweet potato pie, rice and red beans, black beans and rice, pigeon peas and rice, beans and pimentos, spaghetti with Swedish meatballs, codfish and ackee, spinach noodles with clam sauce, five-bean salad, fish salad, and other salads of different combinations.

On gaily decorated trays and platters, a profusion of carefully prepared dishes waited proudly: steamed fish and fried fish and fish pâté, cornbread and succulent collard greens, stir-fry vegetables with ginger and tree ears, startling and deliciously sensual.

There was roti and almond bread, Jamaican harddough bread and sweet rolls, johnnycake and sourdough biscuits. And the punch! A cut-glass punchbowl filled with cassis and mineral water with a blessing of rum, fresh fruit floating seductively on top.

The whole spread reflected a dreamlike fullness of women sharing color and food and warmth and light—*Zami* come true. It filled me with pleasure that such a space could finally come to pass on an icy Tuesday evening in Washington, D.C., and I said so. Majote from Haiti looked exactly like Ginger, and we danced the night down.

January 19, 1984
New York City
I watched the movie *King* on TV tonight, and it brought those days of 1968 vividly back to me—the hope and the pain and the fury and the horror coming so close upon the possibility of change, a bare month after I'd left the Black student poets and my first meeting with Frances, at Tougaloo College in Mississippi. That night at Carnegie Hall when the Tougaloo Choir sang with Duke Ellington. A wealth of promise, of the student singers with their beautiful young Black faces, believing.

I was there to cover the concert for the Jackson, Mississippi, *Clarion Star Ledger.* "What the world needs now is love," they sang. Halfway through the song, the master of ceremonies interrupted to say that Dr. Martin Luther King had just been shot. "What the world needs now is love," they sang, tears lining their faces on stage catching the light, tears rolling down Mr. Honeywell's cheeks. "What the world needs now is love," they sang, his dark rhythmic arms directing the voices through all their weeping. And Dr. King is dead dead dead.

While I watched this movie I was also thinking about the course of my own life, the paths I feel bound for inside myself, the way of life that feels most real to me. And I wonder what I may be risking as I become more and more committed to telling whatever truth comes across my eyes my tongue my pen—no matter how difficult—the world as I see it, people as I feel them. And I wonder what I will have to pay someday for that privilege, and in whose coin? Will those forces which serve non-life in the name of power and profit kill me too, or merely dismember me in the eyes of whoever can use what I do?

When I stand in the radiance of a place like the Sapphire Sapphos dinner, with the elegant food and abundance of love and beautiful dark women, when I stand in that moment of sweetness, I sometimes become almost afraid. Afraid of their warmth and loving, as if that same loving warmth might doom me. I know this is not so, but it can feel like it. As if so long as I remained too different from my own time and surroundings I was safe, if terribly lonely. But now that I am becoming less lonely and more loved, I am also becoming more visible, and therefore more vulnerable. Malcolm saying to Martin in the film, "I love you, Martin, and we are both dead men."

February 9, 1984
New York City

So. No doubt about where we are in the world's story. It has just cost $32,000 to complete a government-commissioned study that purports to show there is no rampant hunger in the U.S.A. I wonder if they realize *rampant* means *aggressive*.

So. The starving old women who used to sit in broken-down rooming houses waiting for a welfare check now lie under park benches and eat out of garbage bins. "I only eat fruit," she mumbled, rummaging through the refuse bin behind Gristedes supermarket, while her gnarled Black hands carefully cut away the rotted parts of a cantaloupe with a plastic Burger King knife.

February 18, 1984
Ohio

How does it *feel*, Ms. L., to be a fifty-year-old Black woman who is still bleeding! Cheers to the years! Doing what I like to do best.

Last night I gave a talk to the Black students at the university about coming to see ourselves as part of an international community of people of Color, how we must train ourselves to question what our Blackness—our Africanness—can mean on the world stage. And how as members of that international community, we must assume responsibility for our actions, or lack of action, as americans. Otherwise, no matter how relative that power might be, we are yielding it up to the opposition to be used against us, and against the forces for liberation around the world. For instance, what are our responsibilities as educated Black women toward the land-rights struggles of other people of Color here and abroad?

I want to write down everything I know about being afraid, but I'd probably never have enough time to write anything else. Afraid is a country where they issue us passports at birth and hope we never seek citizenship in any other country. The face of afraid keeps changing constantly, and I can count on that change. I need to travel light and fast, and there's a lot of baggage I'm going to have to leave behind me. Jettison cargo.

February 19, 1984
New York City

Last night at Blanche and Clare's house was a celebration of my first fifty years. Liz Maybank called—such a wonderful gift to hear her voice across all these years since she helped care for my children. Black Women's Survival 101. I've had many teachers.

Forever is too long to think about. But the future has always been so real to me. Still is. Chances are I don't have liver cancer. No matter what they say. Chances are. That's good. That's bad. Either way I'm a hostage.

So what's new?

Coming to terms with the sadness and the fury. And the curiosity.

March 18, 1984
En route to St. Croix, Virgin Islands

I've written nothing of the intensity with which I've lived the last few weeks. The hepatologist who tried to frighten me into an immediate liver biopsy without even listening to my objections and questions. Seeing the growth in my liver on the CAT scan, doing a face-off with death, again.

Not again, just escalated. This mass in my liver is not a primary liver tumor, so if it is malignant, it's most likely metastasized breast cancer.

Not curable. Arrestable, not curable. This is a very bad dream, and I'm the only person who can wake myself up. I had a talk before I left with Peter, my breast surgeon. He says that if it is liver cancer, with the standard treatments—surgery, radiation, and chemotherapy—we're talking four or five years at best. Without treatment, he says, maybe three or four.

In other words, western medicine doesn't have a very impressive track record with cancer metastasized to the liver.

In the light of those facts, and from all the reading I've been doing these past weeks (thank the goddess for Barnes & Noble's medical section), I've made up my mind not to have a liver biopsy. It feels like the only reasonable decision for me. I'm asymptomatic now except for a vicious gallbladder. And I can placate her. There are too many things I'm determined to do that I haven't done yet. Finish the poem "Outlines." See what europe's all about. Make Deotha Chambers' story live.

If I have this biopsy and it is malignant, then a whole course of action will be established simply by their intrusion into the suspect site.

Yet if this tumor is malignant, I want as much good time as possible, and their treatments aren't going to make a hell of a lot of difference in terms of extended time. But they'll make a hell of a lot of difference in terms of my general condition and how I live my life.

On the other hand, if this is benign, I believe surgical intervention into fatty tissue of any kind can start the malignant process in what otherwise might remain benign for a long time. I've been down that road before.

I've decided this is a chance I have to take. If this were another breast tumor, I'd go for surgery again, because the organ comes off. But with the tie-in between estrogens, fat cells, and malignancies I've been reading about, cutting into my liver seems to me to be too much of a risk for too little return in terms of time. And it might be benign, some little aberrant joke between my liver and the universe.

Twenty-two hours of most days I don't believe I have liver cancer.

Most days. Those other two hours of the day are pure hell, and there's so much work I have to do in my head in those two hours, too, through all the terror and uncertainties.

I wish I knew a doctor I could really trust to talk it all over with. Am I making the right decision? I know I have to listen to my body. If there's one thing I've learned from all the work I've done since my mastectomy, it's that I must listen keenly to the messages my body sends. But sometimes they are contradictory.

Dear goddess! Face-up again against the renewal of vows.

Do not let me die a coward, mother. Nor forget how to sing. Nor forget song is a part of mourning as light is a part of sun.

March 22, 1984
En route to New York City
This was a good trip. Good connections with the Sojourner Sisters and other women in St. Croix. And I finally taught myself to relax in water, swimming about under the sun in Gloria's pool to the sound of Donna Summers blowing across the bright water, "State of Independence," and the coconut tree singing along in the gentle trade winds.

There was a poetry reading last night at the library, with a wide range of age and ability among the poets, but the audience was very responsive.

It reminded me again of how important poetry can be in the life of an ordinary Black community when that poetry is really the poetry of the lives of the people who make up that community.

I suspect I shall have to concentrate upon how painful it is to think about death all the time.

[In the spring of 1984, I spent three months in Berlin conducting a course in Black american women poets and a poetry workshop in English for German students. One of my aims for this trip was to meet Black German women. I'd been told there were quite a few in Berlin, but I had been unable to obtain much information about them in New York.]

May 23, 1984
Berlin, West Germany
Who are they, the German women of the diaspora? Where do our paths intersect as women of Color—beyond the details of

our particular oppressions, although certainly not outside the reference of those details?

And where do our paths diverge? Most important, what can we learn from our connected differences that will be useful to us both, Afro-German and Afro-American?

Afro-German. The women say they've never heard that term used before.

I asked one of my Black students how she'd thought about herself growing up. "The nicest thing they ever called us was 'warbaby,'" she said.

But the existence of most Black Germans has nothing to do with the Second World War, and, in fact, predates it by many decades. I have Black German women in my class who trace their Afro-German heritage back to the 1890s.

For me, Afro-German means the shining faces of Katharina and May in animated conversation about their fathers' homelands, the comparisons, joys, disappointments. It means my pleasure at seeing another Black woman walk into my classroom, her reticence slowly giving way as she explores a new self-awareness, gains a new way of thinking about herself in relation to other Black women.

"I've never thought of Afro-German as a positive concept before," she said, speaking out of the pain of having to live a difference that has no name, speaking out of the growing power self-scrutiny has forged from that difference.

I am excited by these women, by their blossoming sense of identity as they're beginning to say in one way or another, "Let us be ourselves now as we define us. We are not a figment of your imagination or an exotic answer to your desires. We are not some button on the pocket of your longing." I can see these women as a growing force for international change, in concert with other Afro-Europeans, Afro-Asians, Afro-Americans.

We are the hyphenated people of the diaspora whose self-defined identities are no longer shameful secrets in the countries of our origin, but rather declarations of strength and solidarity. We are an increasingly united front from which the world has not yet heard.

June 1, 1984
Berlin

My classes are exciting and exhausting. Black women are hearing about them and their number is increasing.

I can't eat cooked food and I am getting sicker. My liver is so swollen I can feel it under my ribs. I've lost almost fifty pounds. That's a switch, worrying about losing weight. My friend Dagmar, who teaches here, has given me the name of a homeopathic doctor specializing in the treatment of cancer, and I've made an appointment to see her when I come back from the feminist book fair in London next week. She's an anthroposophic doctor, and they believe in surgery only as a last resort.

In spite of all this, I'm doing good work here. I'm certainly enjoying life in Berlin, sick or not. The city itself is very different from what I'd expected. It is lively and beautiful, but its past is never very far away, at least not for me. The silence about Jews is absolutely deafening, chilling.

There is only one memorial in the whole city and it is to the Resistance. At the entrance is a huge grey urn with the sign, "This urn contains earth from German concentration camps." It is such a euphemistic evasion of responsibility and an invitation to amnesia for the children that it's no wonder my students act like Nazism was a bad dream not to be remembered.

There is a lot of networking going on here among women, collectives, and work enterprises as well as political initiatives, and a very active women's cultural scene. I may be too thin, but I can still dance!

June 7, 1984
Berlin

Dr. Rosenberg agrees with my decision not to have a biopsy, but she has said I must do something quickly to strengthen my bodily defenses. She's recommended I begin Iscador injections three times weekly.

Iscador is a biological made from mistletoe which strengthens the natural immune system, and works against the growth of malignant cells. I've started the injections, along with two other herbals that stimulate liver function. I feel less weak.

I am listening to what fear teaches. I will never be gone. I am a scar, a report from the front lines, a talisman, a resurrection. A rough place on the chin of complacency. "What are you getting so upset about, anyway?" a student asked in class. "You're not Jewish!"

So what if I am afraid? Of stepping out into the morning? Of dying?

Of unleashing the damned gall where hatred swims like a tadpole waiting to swell into the arms of war? And what does that war teach when the bruised leavings jump an insurmountable wall where the glorious Berlin chestnuts and orange poppies hide detection wires that spray bullets which kill?

My poems are filled with blood these days because the future is so bloody. When the blood of four-year-old children runs unremarked through the alleys of Soweto, how can I pretend that sweetness is anything more than armor and ammunition in an ongoing war?

I am saving my life by using my life in the service of what must be done. Tonight as I listened to the ANC speakers from

South Africa at the Third World People's Center here, I was filled with a sense of self answering necessity, of commitment as a survival weapon. Our battles are inseparable. Every person I have ever been must be actively enlisted in those battles, as well as in the battle to save my life.

June 9, 1984
Berlin

At the poetry reading in Zurich this weekend, I found it so much easier to discuss racism than to talk about *The Cancer Journals*. Chemical plants between Zurich and Basel have been implicated in a definite rise in breast cancer in this region, and women wanted to discuss this. I talked as honestly as I could, but it was really hard. Their questions presume a clarity I no longer have.

It was great to have Gloria there to help field all those questions about racism. For the first time in europe, I felt I was not alone but answering as one of a group of Black women—not just Audre Lorde!

I am cultivating every iota of my energies to do battle with the possibility of liver cancer. At the same time, I am discovering how furious and resistant some pieces of me are, as well as how terrified.

In this loneliest of places, I examine every decision I make within the light of what I've learned about myself and that self-destructiveness implanted inside of me by racism and sexism and the circumstances of my life as a Black woman.

Mother why were we armed to fight
with cloud wreathed swords and javelins of dust?

Survival isn't some theory operating in a vacuum. It's a matter of my everyday living and making decisions.

How do I hold faith with sun in a sunless place? It is so hard not to counter this despair with a refusal to see. But I have to stay open and filtering no matter what's coming at me, because that arms me in a particularly Black woman's way. When I'm open, I'm also less despairing.

The more clearly I see what I'm up against, the more able I am to fight this process going on in my body that they're calling liver cancer. And I am determined to fight it even when I am not sure of the terms of the battle nor the face of victory. I just know I must not surrender my body to others unless I completely understand and agree with what they think should be done to it. I've got to look at all of my options carefully, even the ones I find distasteful. I know I can broaden the definition of winning to the point where I can't lose.

June 10, 1984
Berlin

Dr. Rosenberg is honest, straightforward, and pretty discouraging. I don't know what I'd do without Dagmar there to translate all her grim pronouncements for me. She thinks it's liver cancer, too, but she respects my decision against surgery. I mustn't let my unwillingness to accept this diagnosis interfere with getting help. Whatever it is, this seems to be working.

We all have to die at least once. Making that death useful would be winning for me. I wasn't supposed to exist anyway, not in any meaningful way in this fucked-up white boys' world. I want desperately to live, and I'm ready to fight for that living even if I die shortly. Just writing those words down snaps everything I want to do into a neon clarity.

This european trip and the Afro-German women, the Sister Outsider collective in Holland, Gloria's great idea of starting an organization that can be a connection between us and South

African women. For the first time I really feel that my writing has a substance and stature that will survive me.

I have done good work. I see it in the letters that come to me about *Sister Outsider*, I see it in the use the women here give the poetry and the prose. But first and last I am a poet. I've worked very hard for that approach to living inside myself, and everything I do, I hope, reflects that view of life, even the ways I must move now in order to save my life.

I have done good work. There is a hell of a lot more I have to do. And sitting here tonight in this lovely green park in Berlin, dusk approaching and the walking willows leaning over the edge of the pool caressing each other's fingers, birds birds birds singing under and over the frogs, and the smell of new-mown grass enveloping my sad pen, I feel I still have enough moxie to do it all, on whatever terms I'm dealt, timely or not.

Enough moxie to chew the whole world up and spit it out in bite-sized pieces, useful and warm and wet and delectable because they came out of my mouth.

June 17, 1984
Berlin
I am feeling more like an Audre I recognize, thank the goddess for Dr. Rosenberg, and for Dagmar for introducing me to her.

I've been reading Christa Wolf 's *The Search for Christa T.*, and finding it very difficult. At first I couldn't grapple with it because it was just too painful to read about a woman dying. Dagmar and a number of the women here in Berlin say the author and I should meet. But now that I'm finished I don't know if I want to meet the woman who wrote it. There is so much pain there that is so far from being felt in any way I recognize or can use, that it makes me very uncomfortable. I feel speechless.

But there is one part of the book that really spoke to me.

In chapter 5, she talks about a mistaken urge to laugh at one's younger self's belief in paradise, in miracles. Each one of us who survives, she says, at least once in our lifetime, at some crucial and inescapable moment, has had to absolutely believe in the impossible. Of course, it occurs to me to ask myself if that's what I'm doing right now, believing in the impossible by refusing a biopsy.

It's been very reassuring to find a medical doctor who agrees with my view of the dangers involved. And I certainly don't reject nondamaging treatment, which is why I'm taking these shots, even though I hate giving myself injections. But that's a small price balanced against the possibility of cancer.

June 20, 1984
Berlin

I didn't go to London because I loved book fairs, but because the idea of the First International Feminist Bookfair excited me, and in particular, I wanted to make contact with the Black feminists of England. Well, the fact remains: the First International Feminist Bookfair was a monstrosity of racism, and this racism coated and distorted much of what was good, creative, and visionary about such a fair. The white women organizers' defensiveness to any question of where the Black women were is rooted in that tiresome white guilt that serves neither us nor them. It reminded me of those old tacky battles of the seventies in the States: a Black woman would suggest that if white women wished to be truly feminist, they would have to examine and alter some of their actions vis-à-vis women of Color. And this discussion would immediately be perceived as an attack upon their very essence. So wasteful and destructive.

I think the organizers of the bookfair really believed that by inviting foreign Black women they were absolving themselves of any fault in ignoring input from local Black women. But we should be able to learn from our errors. They totally objectified *all* Black women by not dealing with the Black women of the London community. Now if anything is to be learned from that whole experience, it should be so that the *next* International Feminist Bookfair does not repeat those errors. And there must be another. But we don't get *there* from *here* by ignoring the mud in between those two positions. If the white women's movement does not learn from its errors, like any other movement, it will die by them. When I stood up for my first reading to a packed house with no Black women's faces, after I'd gotten letter after letter from Black British women asking when was I coming to England, that was the kiss-off. I knew immediately what was up, and the rest is history.

Of course, I was accused of "brutalizing" the organizers by simply asking why Black women were absent. And if my yelling and "jumping up and down" got dirty looks and made white women cry and say all kinds of outrageous nonsense about me, I know it also reinforced other Black women's perceptions about racism here in the women's movement, and contributed to further solidarity among Black women of different communities.

Feminism must be on the cutting edge of real social change if it is to survive as a movement in any particular country. Whatever the core problems are for the people of that country must also be the core problems addressed by women, for we do not exist in a vacuum. We are anchored in our own place and time, looking out and beyond to the future we are creating, and we are part of communities that interact. To pretend otherwise is ridiculous. While we fortify ourselves with visions of the future, we must arm ourselves with accurate perceptions of the barriers between us and that future.

June 21, 1984
Berlin
Rather than siphoning off energies in vain attempts to connect with women who refuse to deal with their own history or ours, Black women need to choose the areas where that energy can be most effective. Who are we? What are the ways in which we do not see each other? And how can we better operate together as a united front even while we explore our differences? Rather than keep yelling at white women's gates, we need to look at our own needs and start giving top priority to satisfying those needs in the service of our joint tasks. How do we deal across our differences of community, time, place, and history? In other words, how do we learn to love each other while we are embattled on so many fronts?

I hope for an International Conference of Black Feminists, asking some of these questions of definition of women from Amsterdam, Melbourne, the South Pacific, Kentucky, New York, and London, all of whom call ourselves Black feminists and all of whom have different strengths.

To paraphrase June Jordan, we are the women we want to become.

August 1, 1984
New York City
Saints be praised! The new CAT scan is unchanged. The tumor has not grown, which means either Iscador is working or the tumor is not malignant!

I feel relieved, vindicated, and hopeful. The pain in my middle is gone, as long as I don't eat very much and stick to fruits and veggies.

That's livable. I feel like a second chance, for true! I'm

making myself a new office upstairs in Jonathan's old room. It's going to be a good year.

October 10, 1984
New York City
I've been thinking about my time in Germany again, unencumbered by artificial shades of terror and self-concern. I don't want my involvement with health matters to obscure the revelation of differences I encountered. The Afro-European women. What I learned about the differences when one teaches about feeling and poetry in a language that is not the original language of the people learning, even when they speak that language fluently. (Of course, all poets learn about feeling as children in our native tongue, and the psychosocial strictures and emotional biases of that language pass over into how we think about feeling for the rest of our lives.) I will never forget the emotional impact of Raja's poetry, and how what she is doing with the German language is so close to what Black poets here are doing with English. It was another example of how our Africanness impacts upon the world's consciousness in intersecting ways.

As an African-American woman, I feel the tragedy of being an oppressed hyphenated person in america, of having no land to be our primary teacher. And this distorts us in so many ways. Yet there is a vital part that we play as Black people in the liberation consciousness of every freedom-seeking people upon this globe, no matter what they say they think about us as Black americans. And whatever our differences are that make for difficulty in communication between us and other oppressed peoples, as Afro-Americans we must recognize the promise we represent for some new social synthesis that the world has not yet experienced. I think of the Afro-Dutch, Afro-German,

Afro-French women I met this spring in europe, and how they are beginning to recognize each other and come together openly in terms of their identities, and I see that they are also beginning to cut a distinct shape across the cultural face of every country where they are at home.

I am thinking about issues of color as color, Black as a chromatic fact, gradations and all. There is the reality of defining Black as a geographical fact of culture and heritage emanating from the continent of Africa—Black meaning Africans and other members of a diaspora, with or without color.

Then there is a quite different reality of defining Black as a political position, acknowledging that color is the bottom line the world over, no matter how many other issues exist alongside it. Within this definition, Black becomes a codeword, a rallying identity for all oppressed people of Color. And this position reflects the empowerment and the worldwide militant legacy of our Black Revolution of the 1960s, the effects of which are sometimes more obvious in other countries than in our own.

I see certain pitfalls in defining Black as a political position. It takes the cultural identity of a widespread but definite group and makes it a generic identity for many culturally diverse peoples, all on the basis of a shared oppression. This runs the risk of providing a convenient blanket of apparent similarity under which our actual and unaccepted differences can be distorted or misused. This blanket would diminish our chances of forming genuine working coalitions built upon the recognition and creative use of acknowledged difference, rather than upon the shaky foundations of a false sense of similarity. When a Javanese Dutch woman says she is Black, she also knows she goes home to another cultural reality that is particular to her people and precious to her—it is Asian, and Javanese. When an African-American woman says she is Black, she is speaking of her cultural reality, no matter how modified it may be by time, place, or circumstances of removal. Yet even the Maori women of New Zealand and the Aboriginal women of Australia call themselves Black. There must be a way for us to deal with this, if only on the level of language. For example, those of us for whom Black is our cultural reality relinquishing the word in favor of some other designation of the African diaspora, perhaps simply *African*.

[The first half of 1985 spins past: a trip to Cuba with a group of Black women writers, a reading tour through the Midwest, the great workspace I created from my son's old room, the beginning of a new collection of poems, my daughter's graduation from college. My general health seemed stable, if somewhat delicate. I removed the question of cancer from my consciousness beyond my regular Iscador treatments, my meager diet, and my lessened energies. In August and September I spent six weeks traveling and giving poetry readings in Australia and New Zealand, a guest of women's groups at various community organizations and universities. It was an exciting and exhausting time, one where thoughts about cancer were constant but never central.]

May 28, 1985
Cambridge, Massachusetts

My daughter Beth's graduation from Harvard this weekend was a rite of passage for both of us. This institution takes itself very seriously, and there was enormous pomp and circumstance for three days. I couldn't help but think of all the racist, sexist ways they've tried through the last four years to diminish and destroy the essence of all the young Black women enrolled here. But it was a very important moment for Beth, a triumph that she'd survived Harvard, that she'd made it out, intact, and in a self she can continue living with. Of course, the point of so much of what goes on at places like Harvard—supposed to be about learning—is actually geared to either destroying these young people, or altering their substance into effigies that will be pliant, acceptable, and nonproblematic to the system. So I was proud of Beth standing there in the manicured garden of Adams House, wearing her broad white Disinvestment banner across her black commencement gown, but I was also very scared for her. Out there can be even more difficult, although now she knows at least that she can and did survive Harvard. And with her own style unimpaired.

I embarrassed myself because I kept trying to find secret places to cry in, but it was still a very emotionally fulfilling occasion. I feel she's on her way now in a specific sense that must leave me behind, and that is both sad and very reassuring to me. I am convinced that Beth has the stuff—the emotional and psychic wherewithal to do whatever she needs to do for her living, and I have given her the best I have to offer. I remember writing "What My Child Learns of the Sea" when she was three months old, and it's both terrifying and wonderful to see it all coming true. I bless the goddess that I am still here to see it.

I tremble for her, for them all, because of the world we are giving them and all the work still to be done, and the gnawing question of will there be enough time? But I celebrate her, too, another one of those fine, strong, young Black women moving out to war, outrageous and resilient, plucky and beautiful.

I'm proud of her, and I'm proud of having seen her this far. It's a relief for me to know that whatever happens with my health now, and no matter how short my life may be, she is essentially on her way in the world, and next year Jonathan will be stepping out with his fine self, too.

I look at them and they make my heart sing. Frances and I have done good work.

August 10, 1985
Melbourne, Australia
A group of white Australian women writers invited me to give the keynote address on "The Language of Difference" at a women's writing conference held in Melbourne as part of the 150-year celebration of the founding of the state of Victoria. These are my remarks:

> I am here upon your invitation, a Black African-American woman speaking of the language of difference. We come together in this place on the 150th anniversary of the state of Victoria, an Australian state built upon racism, destruction, and a borrowed sameness. We were never meant to speak together at all. I have struggled for many weeks to find your part in me, to see what we could share that would have meaning for us all. When language becomes most similar, it becomes most dangerous, for then differences may pass unremarked. As women of good faith we can only become familiar with the language of difference within a determined commitment to its use within our lives, without romanticism and without guilt. Because we share a common language which is not of our own making and which does not reflect our deeper knowledge as women, our words frequently sound the same. But it is an error to believe that we mean the same experience, the same commitment, the same future, unless we agree to examine the history and particular passions that lie beneath each other's words.

When I say I am Black, I mean I am of African
descent. When I say I am a woman of Color, I mean I
recognize common cause with American Indian,
Chicana, Latina, and Asian-American sisters of North
America. I also mean I share common cause with
women of Eritrea who spend most of each day searching
for enough water for their children, as well as with
Black South African women who bury 50 percent of
their children before they reach the age of five. And I
also share cause with my Black sisters of Australia, the
Aboriginal women of this land who were raped of their
history and their children and their culture by a
genocidal conquest in whose recognition we are gath-
ered here today.

I have reached down deep inside of me to find what it
was we could share, and it has been very difficult,
because I find my tongue weighted down by the blood of
my Aboriginal sisters that has been shed upon this
earth. For the true language of difference is yet to be
spoken in this place. Here that language must be spoken
by my Aboriginal sisters, the daughters of those indige-
nous peoples of Australia with whom each one of you
shares a destiny, but whose voices and language most of
you here have never heard.

One hundred and fifty years ago, when the state of
Victoria was declared a reality for european settlers,
there were still 15,000 Black Aboriginal people living on
this land that is now called Victoria. Where we sit now
today, Wurundjeri women once dreamed and laughed
and sang. They nurtured this earth, gum tree and wattle,
and they were nurtured by it. I do not see their daughters
sitting here among you today. Where are these women?

Their mothers' blood cries out to me. Their daughters come to my dreams nightly in the Windsor Hotel across the street from your Parliament. And their voices are haunting and brave and sad. Do you hear them? Listen very carefully, with your hearts open. They are speaking. Out of their mouths come what you have said you most want to hear.

Their history is my history. While white immigrant settlers in Australia were feeding Wurundjeri women and children bread made from arsenic and flour, white immigrant settlers in North America were selling seven-year-old African girls for $35 a head. And these same white immigrant settlers were giving blankets lethal with smallpox germs to the indigenous peoples of North America, the American Indians.

Each of you has come here today to touch some piece of your own power, for a purpose. I urge you to approach that work with a particular focus and urgency, for a terrible amount of Wurundjeri women's blood has already been shed in order for you to sit and write here.

I do not say these things to instigate an orgy of guilt, but rather to encourage an examination of what the excavation and use of the true language of difference can mean within your living. You and I can talk about the language of difference, but that will always remain essentially a safe discussion, because this is not my place. I will move on. But it is the language of the Black Aboriginal women of this country that you must learn to hear and to feel. And as your writing and your lives intersect within that language, you will come to decide what mistress your art must serve.

October 24, 1985
East Lansing, Michigan

Tomorrow is the second anniversary of the invasion of Grenada. The smallest nation in the western hemisphere occupied by the largest. I spoke about it to a group of Black women here tonight. It's depressing to see how few of us remember, how few of us still seem to care.

The conference on "The Black Woman Writer and the Diaspora" being held here is problematic in some ways, particularly in the unclear position of Ellen Kuzwayo, who had come all the way from South Africa to give the keynote address and arrived here to find the schedule shifted. But it was so good to see Ellen again. I'm sorry to hear her sister in Botswana has had another mastectomy.

It's been very exciting to sit down with African and Caribbean women writers whom I've always wanted to meet. Octavia Butler is here also, and Andrea Canaan from New Orleans. I haven't seen her in over a year, and the look in her eyes when she saw me made me really angry, but it also made me realize how much weight I've lost in the past year and how bad my color's been since I came home from Australia. I've got to go see Dr. C. for a checkup when I get home.

October 25, 1985
East Lansing

I gave a brief talk tonight on "Sisterhood and Survival," what it means to me. And first off I identified myself as a Black Feminist Lesbian poet, although it felt unsafe, which is probably why I had to do it. I explained that I identified myself as such because if there was one other Black Feminist Lesbian poet in isolation somewhere within the reach of my voice, I wanted her to know she was not alone. I think a lot about Angelina Weld Grimké, a Black Lesbian poet of the Harlem Renaissance who is never identified as such, when she is mentioned at all, although the work of Gloria Hull and Erlene Stetson recently has focused renewed attention upon her. But I never even knew her name when I was going to school, and later, she was the briefest of mentions in a list of "other" Harlem Renaissance writers.

I often think of Angelina Weld Grimké dying alone in an apartment in New York City in 1958 while I was a young Black Lesbian struggling in isolation at Hunter College, and I think of what it could have meant in terms of sisterhood and survival for each one of us to have known of the other's existence: for me to have had her words and her wisdom, and for her to have known I needed them! It is so crucial for each one of us to know she is not alone. I've been traveling a lot in the last two years since my children are grown, and I've been learning what an enormous amount I don't know as a Black american woman. And wherever I go, it's been so heartening to see women of Color reclaiming our lands, our heritages, our cultures, our selves—usually in the face of enormous odds.

For me as an African-American woman writer, sisterhood and survival means it's not enough to say I believe in peace when my sisters' children are dying in the streets of Soweto and New Caledonia in the South Pacific. Closer to home, what are we as Black women saying to our sons and our nephews and our students as they are, even now, being herded into the military by unemployment and despair, someday to become meat in the battles to occupy the lands of other people of Color?

How can we ever, ever forget the faces of those young Black american soldiers, their gleaming bayonets drawn, staking out a wooden shack in the hills of Grenada? What is our real work as Black women writers of the diaspora? Our responsibilities to other Black women and their children across this globe we share, struggling for our joint future? And what if our sons are someday ordered into Namibia, or Southwest Africa, or Zimbabwe, or Angola?

Where does our power lie and how do we school ourselves to use it in the service of what we believe?

Sitting with Black women from all over the earth has made me think a great deal about what it means to be indigenous, and what my relationship as a Black woman in North America is to the land-rights struggles of the indigenous peoples of this land, to Native American Indian women, and how we can translate that consciousness into a new level of working together. In other words, how can we use each other's differences in our common battles for a livable future?

All of our children are prey. How do we raise them not to prey upon themselves and each other? And this is why we cannot be silent, because our silences will come to testify against us out of the mouths of our children.

November 21, 1985
New York City

It feels like the axe is falling. There it is on the new CAT scan—another mass growing in my liver, and the first one is spreading. I've found an anthroposophic doctor in Spring Valley who suggests I go to the Lukas Klinik, a hospital in Switzerland where they are conducting the primary research on Iscador, as well as diagnosing and treating cancers.

I've known something is wrong from the returning pains and the dimming energies of my body. My classes have been difficult, and most days I feel like I'm going on sheer will power alone which can be very freeing and seductive but also very dangerous. Limited. I'm running down. But I'd do exactly what I'm doing anyway, cancer or no cancer.

A. will lend us the money to go to Switzerland, and Frances will come with me. I think they will be able to find out what is really wrong with me at the Lukas Klinik, and if they say these growths in my liver are malignant, then I will accept that I have cancer of the liver. At least there they will be able to adjust my Iscador dosage upward to the maximum effect, because that is the way I have decided to go and I'm not going to change now. Obviously, I still don't accept these tumors in my liver as cancer, although I know that could just be denial on my part, which is certainly one mechanism for coping with cancer. I have to consider denial as a possibility in all of my planning, but I also feel that there is absolutely nothing they can do for me at Sloane [sic] Kettering except cut me open and then sew me back up with their condemnations inside me.

December 7, 1985
New York City
My stomach x-rays are clear, and the problems in my GI series are all circumstantial. Now that the doctors here have decided I have liver cancer, they insist on reading all their findings as if that were a fait accompli.

They refuse to look for any other reason for the irregularities in the x-rays, and they're treating my resistance to their diagnosis as a personal affront. But it's my body and my life and the goddess knows I'm paying enough for all this, I ought to have a say.

The flame is very dim these days. It's all I can do to teach my classes at Hunter and crawl home. Frances and I will leave for Switzerland as soon as school is over next week. The Women's

Poetry Center will be dedicated at Hunter the night before I leave. No matter how sick I feel, I'm still afire with a need to do something for my living. How will I be allowed to live my own life, the rest of my life?

December 9, 1985
New York City
A better question is—how do I want to live the rest of my life and what am I going to do to ensure that I get to do it exactly or as close as possible to how I want that living to be?

I want to live the rest of my life, however long or short, with as much sweetness as I can decently manage, loving all the people I love, and doing as much as I can of the work I still have to do. I am going to write fire until it comes out my ears, my eyes, my noseholes—everywhere. Until it's every breath I breathe. I'm going to go out like a fucking meteor!

December 13, 1985
New York City
There are some occasions in life too special to dissect, not only because they are everything they are supposed to be, but because they are also a sum of unexpected fantasies and deep satisfactions all come together at one point in time. Tonight the students of the Hunter College Women's Poetry Center Club and the *Returning Woman Newsletter* dedicated the Audre Lorde Women's Poetry Center. Walking into that hall, even thirty minutes late, was the beginning of exactly that kind of evening, and nothing I nor anyone else will ever do can lessen its meaning for me. Whatever happens to me, there has been a coming together in time and space of some of my best efforts, hopes, and desires. There is a tangible possibility to be built

upon and strong young women committed to doing it. I wish them the power of their vision for what this center can be in their lives and in the life of a community of women's culture in this city, the vision of a living women's poetry as a force for social change. This evening brought together four of my deepest and longest-lasting interests—poetry, beautiful women, revolution, and me!

No matter what I find out in Switzerland, no matter what's going on in my body, this is my work. The recognition of it, the sweet strength and love in the faces tonight make me know how much what I do has meant to these women who are arming themselves to walk in places I've only dreamed of, and in their own step and as their own mistresses.

I listened tonight to these young poets, particularly the women of Color, reading their work, and it was wonderful for me to know that the real power of my words is not the pieces of me that reside within those words, but the life force—the energy and aspirations and desires at the complex core of each one of these women—which has been aroused to use and to answer my words. Gloria, Johnnetta, and I—three of the founding mothers of the Sisterhood in Support of Sisters in South Africa—within that precious space where we sit down together in my intricate life. The young poets shining like gold fire in the sun, their many-colored faces awash with pride and determination and love. Beth and Yolanda, daughter and old friend, my words coming out of their mouths illuminated exactly by who they are themselves, so different from each other and from me. The revelation of hearing my work translated through the beings of these women I love so dearly. Frances, smiling like a sunflower and really there; my sister Helen looking pleased and a part of it all; and Mabel Hampton, tough and snappy and hanging in, all eighty-three years of her!

Charlotte's[*] generous perfume, and I remember the sureness in her voice once, saying, "Well, we did what we had to do, and I think we changed the world!" Alexis[†] and her twinkling eyes, Clare's[‡] warm graciousness. And Blanchie,[§] resplendent and cheeky in her tuxedo, orchestrating it all with her particular special flair, mistress of ceremonies to quite a party!

December 15, 1985
Arlesheim, Switzerland
So here I am at the Lukas Klinik while my body decides if it will live or die. I'm going to fight like hell to make it live, and this looks like the most promising possibility. At least it's something different from narcotics and other terminal aids, which is all Dr. C. had to offer me in New York City in lieu of surgery when I told her how badly I hurt in my middle. "Almost everything I eat now makes me sick," I told her. "Yes, I know," she said sorrowfully, writing me a prescription for codeine and looking at me as if there was nothing left she could do for me besides commiserate. Even though I like her very much, I wanted to punch her in her mouth.

I have found something interesting in a book here on active meditation as a form of self-control. There are six steps:

1. Control of Thought
   Think of a small object (i.e., a paper clip) for five minutes, exclusively. Practice for a month.

---

[*] Ex-slave who led a workers' revolt in St. Croix in 1848.
[†] Alexis De Veaux, poet and biographer.
[‡] Clare Cross, playwright, psychotherapist, and partner of Blanche Cook.
[§] Blanche Cook, classmate of Lorde at Hunter College, historian, and partner of Clare Cross.

2. Control of Action
   Perform a small act every day at the same time. Practice, and be patient.
3. Control of Feeling (equanimity)
   Become aware of feelings and introduce equanimity into experiencing them—i.e., be afraid, not panic-stricken. (They're big on this one around here.)
4. Positivity (tolerance)
   Refrain from critical downgrading thoughts that sap energy from good work.
5. Openness (receptivity)
   Perceive even what is unpleasant in an unfettered, non-prejudiced way.
6. Harmony (perseverance)
   Work toward balancing the other five.

As a living creature I am part of two kinds of forces—growth and decay, sprouting and withering, living and dying—and at any given moment of our lives, each one of us is actively located somewhere along a continuum between these two forces.

December 16, 1985
Arlesheim

I brought some of my books with me, and reading *The Cancer Journals* in this place is like excavating words out of the earth, like turning up a crystal that has been buried at the bottom of a mine for a thousand years, waiting. Even *Our Dead Behind Us*—now that it has gone to the printer—seems prophetic. Like always, it feels like I plant what I will need to harvest, without consciousness.

This is why the work is so important. Its power doesn't lie in the me that lives in the words so much as in the heart's blood pumping behind the eye that is reading, the muscle behind the desire that is sparked by the word—hope as a living state that propels us, open-eyed and fearful, into all [of] the battles of our lives. And some of those battles we do not win.

But some of them we do.

December 17, 1985
Arlesheim

When I read in Basel last June, I never imagined I would be here again, four miles away, in a hospital. I remember the women in the bookstore that night, and their questions about survival rates that I could not answer then. And certainly not now.

Even in the bleak Swiss winter, the grounds of the Lukas Klinik are very beautiful. Much care has been given by the builders to the different shades of winter scenery, so there is a play of light and dark that hits the eye from the room's windows as well as from the beds. My private room is good-sized, spacious by american hospital standards. It is one of the few single rooms with a private bath, and they are usually for very sick or very rich people. I think the administration was not sure which category I fit into when I called from New York.

Even when it is not sunny, the room is light because everything in it is light. Not white, except for the bedsheets, but very light. Even the furniture is solid hand-hewn blond wood, made in one of the sheltered workshops run in conjunction with an anthroposophic school for developmentally handicapped people. The Rudolf Steiner schools have had great success in the area of special education.

There is a deep serenity here, relaxing and sometimes uncomfortable. The adjustable hospital bed is covered with a voluptuous down comforter under which a hot-water bottle had been slipped the first night I arrived. And six red rosebuds in a cut-glass vase. On the other side of the bedside table is an easy chair, and then a wide window and a glass door opening onto terraces that run the length of each of the tiered three stories of the building. The tiers provide plenty of sunlight on each floor. There are opaque dividers for privacy between the doors leading onto the terrace, and then a common strollway open to the sky.

Beneath the terraces is a carefully tended european garden, sculptured stone steps cut into one side winding back and forth through the low bushes and plantings throughout the grounds. In the grassy clearing in front of the terraces stands a red granite statue of a robed person with what I have come to think of as the Steiner look, blunt and massive, one arm upraised in the eurhythmic position for the vowel *i* which is considered in all languages to be the sound representing the affirmation of self in living. On a slight knoll, the statue is silhouetted against the green trees or the leaden sky.

At the foot of the statue and to one side is a large oval whirlpool fountain of red granite also, its perennial gurgle of softly flowing water a soothing counterpoint whenever the terrace door is opened, or when walking through the grounds.

A quite lovely pastel painting of a sunrise hangs on one wall of the room, executed according to the Rudolf Steiner theory of color and healing. It is the only wall decoration in the room, whose walls are painted a sunny yellow and peach.

Most of the patients are middle-aged Swiss and Germans, with two French women and myself. We all wear our own clothes. There is a large sitting room that contains a library, and a chapel, of course, and appropriate Steiner reading materials [are] always available.

Everyone who works with patients gives off a similar affect: it is calm, kind, and helpful, but also completely dogmatic. Staff, patients, and visitors eat lunch and dinner together in a spacious, well-draped but sunny dining room with real linens and individualized embroidered napkins. We are seated at tables holding six to ten diners, amid signs of the zodiac and planets sculpted from various kinds of european bedrock, also done in the Steiner artistic tradition of massive, solid lines.

Meals are a real chore for me, since it is difficult for me to eat anyway and I loathe eating around strangers. The feeling in the dining room is genteel, cultivated, and totally formal.

I take a one-and-a-half-hour class daily in curative eurhythmy with a tiny East Indian woman named Dilnawaz who was raised in Rudolf Steiner schools in India, trained in Germany, and speaks fluent English and German as well as her native tongue.

Eurhythmy is a combination of sustained rhythmical body movements and controlled breathing, based upon vowel and consonant sounds. As I learn and practice the stylized movements, they remind me of tai chi and feel like a complement to the Simonton visualization work I've been doing for a while. My body feels relaxed and good after eurhythmy, and my mind, too.

There is a part of me that wants to dismiss everything here other than Iscador as irrelevant or at least not useful to me, even before I try it, but I think that is very narrow and counterproductive and I don't want to do it. At least not without first giving myself fully to it, because that is why I came all this way and what do I have to lose at this point? Dilnawaz stresses that the treatment of any disease, and of cancer in particular, must be all of a piece, body and mind, and I am ready to try anything so long as they don't come at me with a knife.

Dilnawaz is the most human, the most friendly, and the most real person I've met here, as well as the most spiritual. She is also the most lonely. She is very friendly and helpful toward everyone, and people respond to her with considerable respect, but there is still an air of isolation about her that says to me she is not quite a part. She lives alone in Arlesheim town, and her sister is coming from Germany to spend Christmas with her.

I wonder how she feels as a woman of Color among all these white ethnocentric Swiss. She is very cautious about what she says, but she does talk of how reluctant most northern europeans are to give themselves to eurhythmy. I find her a touch of emotional color within a scene of extraordinary blandness.

Dilnawaz seems to be relieved to see me, too. I think she knows I have a deep respect for the spiritual aspect of our lives and its power over us. That is something most of the rationalists here do not have, despite their adherence to Steiner's anthroposophy. It seems they can only deal with spirituality if it comes with rigid rules imposed from the outside, i.e., Steiner, with his insistence upon the basic rule of a Christian god. It is limiting.

I take a class in painting and color theory according to Steiner. Afterward, an oil dispersion bath which alternates with a massage (also according to Steiner), then lunch, a hot yarrow liver poultice, and a two hour rest period. Then I am free until dinner, unless there are medical consultations or tests. This is when Frances and I get to see each other privately for a while.

There are about fifty patients here right now, and about fifteen doctors, as well as some visiting doctors and medical trainees from different countries. The calm directness with which everyone seems to deal with the idea and reality of disease is quite unlike anything I've experienced in hospitals in the U.S., given that all the patients here either have cancer or are suspected of having cancer. At its best, the effect of this directness is very calming and reassuring, very centering. At its worst, it feels like Mann's *Magic Mountain*. Because at the same time, nobody believes in talking about feelings, even the strong expression of which is considered to be harmful, or at least too stressful to be beneficial.

In the private room next door to me, there is a pretty young Swiss woman of no more than twenty, with a gold wedding band on and very expensive clothes and too much make-up. She appears terribly depressed all the time. Evidently she goes to church in town every morning, because I see her passing through the grounds early each day wearing a church cap. Her family seems very rich or very influential. They came to visit yesterday, and I saw them in the dining room—mother, father, and a young man who was either brother or husband. They sure looked rich, and everyone here bowed and scraped to them. (The social hierarchy is quite strongly observed.) It seems to me that anyone that young who has cancer must be filled with rage and should at least be able to talk about her feelings with someone. But that's not considered necessary or beneficial here.

There is an elderly woman schoolteacher from Hamburg who wears a beautifully carved rhodonite necklace to lunch every day. We have had an interesting conversation about rocks and minerals, which are considered to be very important and powerful in anthroposophy. She speaks English quite well and tries to be friendly. She has been an anthroposoph for many years, she says, and this is her second stay at the Klinik.

The most frequent question from English-speaking patients and medical trainees, couched in different ways, is: how does an american—and a Black one at that, although the latter is only inferred because everyone here is much too well-bred and polite to ever let on they notice, although Sister Maria did tell me yesterday that her brother is a missionary in South Africa so she understands why I like to eat raw vegetables—how does an american come to be at the Lukas Klinik in Switzerland? americans are known for being quite provincial.

One of the cardinal rules here is that we do not talk about our illness at mealtimes or at any social gathering, so everyone is very polite and small-talky and banal, because of course we are all preoccupied with our bodies and the processes going on within them or else we wouldn't be here. I don't know what makes the anthroposophs think this sort of false socializing is not more stressful than expressing real feelings, but I find it terribly wearing. Mercifully, I can usually retreat behind the language barrier.

December 19, 1985
Arlesheim
I sit lie paint walk dance weep in a Swiss hospital trying to find out what my body wants to do, waiting for doctors to come talk with me. Last night my stomach and liver cried all night. "So this is the way of dying," I thought, my body feeling almost transparent. In the sunlight now I think someone was dying next door, and I felt the sadness through the walls coupled with my own. When the sun came up I felt a lot better, until I saw the bed stripped down in the hallway, and the next-door buzzer silent at last.

The village of Arlesheim is very lovely and picturesque. Frances and I go for long walks in the park holding hands in our coat pockets, giving each other courage, and wondering about the future. I have written no letters, no poems, no journals except these notes, trying to make sense out of it all.

I am often in pain and I fear that it will get worse. I need to sharpen every possible weapon against it, but even more so against the fear, or the fear of fear, which is what is so debilitating. And I want to learn how to do that while there is still time for learning in some state before desperation. Desperation. Reckless through despair.

There is no more time left to decide upon strange afflictions.

December 20, 1985
Arlesheim

A men's choir from the village sang Christmas carols tonight in the hospital stairwells, their voices echoing through the halls, sweet and poignant, and I cried for Christmases I have had that are past. But I simply cannot allow myself to believe that there will never be any more of them, so there surely must be. How different this season is from any holiday season I could possibly have foreseen. Dear goddess! How many more?

Frances' being here makes it complete in an essential way no matter what, and at least we can wander about the village in the afternoons together looking at the shops, or walk the hills enjoying the countryside and the manicured little winter gardens. I stretch to be able to appreciate the loveliness in its own—european—right, before it is gone, too, and I no longer have a chance to explore it for whatever it can mean for me.

December 21, 1985
Arlesheim

I sleep well here when I sleep. Yesterday was another horrendous communal dinner. Difficult as it is for me to get anything down, I find the genteel smugness, the sameness, infuriating. It's better now that Frances has started taking her meals here with me. At least we can talk to each other.

I had to do battle between the soup and the salad with an Australian pig who proved that racism is as alive and well in Arlesheim as it was on that wretched bus in Melbourne when that drunken Aussie accosted me thinking I was *Koori* (Aborigine).

The choir really got to me tonight, mellow and measured and very civilized, so long as you accept their terms of living and their way of life and values. The sweet voices, the smell of pine, and the lovely candle arrangements with red and green holly in every hallway, the Christmas decorations in all the corridors, the determined cheerfulness. Nurses go around and open every door a bit so that everyone can hear the music. Soft lights shining in the twilight windows. Very lovely. Just don't be different. Don't even think about being different. It's bad for you.

Today is the day the sun returns. Sweet Solstice. Mother, arm me for whatever is ahead of me. Let me at the very least be equal to it, if not totally in charge of changing it. Last night Gloria called. As she said, take whatever you can use there and let the rest go.

Another choir is singing now in the halls. If I had the strength, I would get up from this bed and run out into the starlit freezing night and keep running until I collapsed into a heap of huffs and puffs of effort and strained muscles. But I can't quite manage that, and Frances has gone back to her hotel, and my heart aches from strangeness. The sound of these voices singing familiar melodies in a foreign tongue only reminds me of the distance between me and my familiar places.

Yet this is the only place I know right now that offers me any hope, and that will treat me and my liver seriously.

December 22, 1985
Arlesheim

I have brought some of my stones and macramé threads with me. I've laid out the stones on my windowsill, and they are beautiful in the light. I'm going to make a new healing necklace for myself from them while I'm here, and I'm going to make the heart-piece from carnelian, which is a specific against melancholy. And that's my answer to Sister Marie's cautioning me against the dangers of an excess of joy!

It's the nights after Frances goes back to the hotel that are the hardest. I spend my day racing around between those dreadful public meals and the eurhythmics and painting and baths and tests and running over to Frances' hotel for a quick cuddle then back here for a liver compress or to take my temperature or something else equally vital in this half-seen scheme of things that feels like a pact I've made with myself to do as they believe is best for a stated period of time—three weeks. In other words, to give the Lukas Klinik my best shot because it is the only thing I have going for me right now, and tomorrow the results from all my liver tests and other diagnostic analyses will be back. I haven't really thought about what they will be because I just can't spend any more energy in being scared.

What I have to fight the hardest against here is feeling that it is just not worth it—too much fight for too little return, and I hurt all the damn time. Something is going on inside me, and it's interfering with my life. There is a persistent and pernicious despair hovering over me constantly that feels physiological, even when my basic mood is quite happy. I don't understand it, but I do not want to slip or fall into any kind of resignation. I am not going to go gently into anybody's damn good night!

December 23, 1985, 10:30 a.m.
Arlesheim

I have cancer of the liver.

Dr. Lorenz just came in and told me. The crystallization test and the liver sonogram are all positive. The two masses in my liver are malignant. He says I should begin an increased Iscador program and antihormone therapy right away, if I decide that is the way I want to go. Well. The last possibility of doubt based on belief is gone. I said I'd come to Lukas because I trusted the anthroposophic doctors, and if they said it was malignant then I would accept their diagnosis. So here it is, and all the yelling and head-banging isn't going to change it. I guess it helps to finally know. I wish Frances were here.

I cannot afford to waste any more time in doubting, or in fury. The question is, what do I do now? Listen to my body, of course, but the messages get dimmer and dimmer. In two weeks I go back home. Iscador or chemotherapy or both?

How did I ever come to be in this place? What can I use it for?

December 24, 1985
Arlesheim
I feel trapped on a lonely star. Someone else is very sick next door, and the vibes are almost too painful to bear. But I must stop saying that now so glibly. Someday something will, in fact, be too painful to bear and then I will have to act. Does one simply get tired of living? I can't imagine right now what that would be like, but that is because I feel filled with a fury to live—because I believe life can be good even when it is painful—a fury that my energies just don't match my desires anymore.

December 25, 1985
Arlesheim
Good morning, Christmas. A Swiss bubble is keeping me from talking to my children and the women I love. The front desk won't put my calls through. Nobody here wants to pierce this fragile, delicate bubble that is the best of all possible worlds, they

believe. So frighteningly insular. Don't they know good things get better by opening them up to others, giving and taking and changing? Most people here seem to feel that rigidity is a bona fide pathway to peace, and every fiber of me rebels against that.

December 26, 1985
Arlesheim

Adrienne [Rich] and Michelle [Cliff] and Gloria [Joseph] just called from California. I feel so physically cut off from the people I love. I need them, the sharing of grief and energy.

I am avoiding plunging directly into the nightmare of liver cancer as a fact of my life by edging into it like an icy bath. I am trying to edge my friends into it, too, without having to deal with more of their fury and grief than I can handle. There is some we share, and that mutual support makes us closer and more resolved. But there is some that they will have to deal with on their own, just as there is some fury and grief that I can only meet in a private place. Frances has been so true and staunch here. It is more difficult for her sometimes because she does not have the fount of desperate determination that survival is generating inside me.

There is so much to keep track of. I think it's crucial that I not only suffer this but record, in the fullness and the lean, some of the raw as well as digested qualities of now.

Last night there was a Christmas full moon, and it felt like a hopeful sign. I stood out in the road in front of the hospital under the full moon on Christmas night and thought about all of my beloved people, the women I love, my children, my family, all the dear faces before my eyes. The moon was so clear and bright, I could feel her upon my skin through Helen's fur coat.

After I had gone to bed she called me back to her twice.

The first time I could not pierce through the veil of sleep, but I saw her light and heard her in my dreams. Then at 4:30 in the morning, her little fingers of light reached under the lined window curtains, and I got up as if bidden and went out onto the terrace to greet her. The night was very very still; she was low and bright and brilliantly clear. I stood on the terrace in my robe bathed in her strong quiet light. I raised my arms then and prayed for us all, prayed for the strength for all of us who must weather this time ahead with me. My mother moon had awakened me, calling me out into her brightness, and she shone down upon me as a sign, a blessing on that terrace with the soft gurgle of flowing water in my ears, a promise of answering strength to be whoever I need to be. I felt her in my heart, in my bones, in my thin blood, and I heard Margareta's voice again: "It's going to be a hard lonely road, but remember, help is on the way." That was her farewell Tarot reading for me, seventeen years ago.

December 27, 1985
Arlesheim
Last night I dreamed I was asleep here in my bed at the Klinik and there was a strange physical presence lying beside me on the left side. I couldn't see it because it was dark, but I felt this body start to touch me on my left thigh, and I knew that this meant great danger. "It must think I'm dead so it can have (claim) me," I thought, "but if I moan it will know I'm awake and alive and it'll leave me alone." So I began to moan softly, but the creature didn't stop. I could feel its cold fingers beginning to creep over my left hip, and I thought to myself, "Oh, oh, nightmare time! I've got to scream louder. Maybe that noise will make it go away, because there is nobody else here to wake

me up!" So I screamed and roared in my sleep, and finally after what seemed like a very long time, I woke myself up calling out, and of course there was nothing in my bed at all, but it still felt as if death had really been trying.

December 30, 1985
Arlesheim

Frances and I went to the Konditorei [pastry shop] in town this afternoon to have a cup of tea and be together away from the hospital, when the elderly schoolteacher with the rhodonite necklace came in and wanted to sit down with us. It was so apparent how badly she wanted to talk that we couldn't say no, even though we never have enough time alone together.

It was actually quite sad. Dr. Lorenz had just told her that her breast cancer has spread to her bones, and she doesn't know what she is going to do. She has to make plans for her elderly mother for whom she now cares at home but will no longer be able to. There is no one she knows to whom she can turn for help because her sister died last year. I felt very sorry for her. Here it is, almost New Year's Eve, and there isn't even anyone she can talk to about her worries except two strange americans in a tea shop.

Then she went on to explain that she and her sister had had to live with foreign workers (she meant Italians) in the factory where they worked during World War II, and that the foreigners were very dirty, with lice and fleas, so she and her sister would sprinkle DDT in their hair and their beds every night so as not to catch diseases! And she is sure that is why the cancer has spread to her bones now. There was something so grotesque about this sad lonely old woman dying of bone cancer still holding on to her ethnic prejudices, even when she was realizing that they were going to cost her her life. The image of her as a young healthy aryan bigot was at war inside me with the pathetic old woman at our table, and I had to get out of there immediately.

December 31, 1985
Arlesheim

Old Year's Day, the last day of this troubled year. And yes, all the stories we tell are about healing in some form or the other.

In this place that makes such a point of togetherness and community, Frances and I sat through an ornate New Year's Eve dinner tonight surrounded by empty chairs on each side of us, an island unto ourselves in the festive hall. It's good that we have each other, but why should I have to suffer through this ostracism and pay for it as well? I guess because the point is not that I enjoy it but that I gain from it, and that's up to me. As Gloria said on the phone, "Take what you can use and let the rest GO!" They don't have to love me, just help me.

My Maori jade tiki is gone forever, either lost or stolen from my room. How much more do I have to lose before it is enough?

I cannot bear to think that this might be my last New Year's Eve. But it might be. What a bummer! But if that's true at least I have had others which were sweet and full past comparing, and filled with enough love and promise to last forever and beyond me. Frances, Beth and Jonathan, Helen, Blanche and Clare, our loving circle. I hold now to what I know and have always known in my heart ever since I first knew what loving was—that when it truly exists it is the most potent and lasting force in life, even if certainly not the fastest. But without it nothing else is worth a damn.

After Frances went back to the hotel I washed my hair (wishing I had some white flowers to put in the water for a blessing), listened to Bob Marley, and went to bed.

January 1, 1986
Arlesheim

Today Frances and I hiked to the top of a mountain to see the Dornach ruins, and the whole Rhine valley spread out beneath us. It felt so good to be moving my body again. My mother always used to say that whatever you do on New Year's Day you will do all year round, and I'd certainly like to believe that's true.

It was very cold and sunny and bright, three miles up and back. The ruins rang with that historical echo and the presence of trials labored and past, although not as profoundly as the stones of El Morro in Cuba, and certainly not as desperately as the walls of Elmina Castle in Ghana, from whence so many Black women and children and men were sent to hell—slavery.

February 20, 1986
Anguilla, British West Indies

I am here seeking sun on my bones. A dry little island with outlandishly beautiful beaches, and soft-voiced West Indian people living their lives by the sea. Anguilla's primary source of income is from import duties, second comes fishing. I go out at dawn to see the fishermen put out from Crocus Bay, and when they return they sometimes give Gloria and me fish. An intricate network of ownership and shares governs the dividing up of each catch.

Fossilized sand dollars wash out of the sand banks onto the beaches of Anguilla and out of the claystone bluffs that grade downward toward the beach. I spend hours wandering the beaches and searching for them, or collecting shells that I rinse at the water's green edge. I would never have known about this island except for Gloria. Anguilla feels like a piece of home, a very healing, restful place, but with the rich essences of life.

The sun and the sea here are helping me save my life. They

are a far softer cry from the East River, Spuyten Duyvil, and the lower New York Bay. But always, the sea speaks to me no matter where I get to her. I suppose that is a legacy of my mother's, from when we used to stand, all those years ago, staring out over the sooty pebbles at the foot of 142nd Street and the Harlem River. Anguilla reminds me of Carriacou, the tiny island off the coast of Grenada where my mother was born.

When I am next to the sea, the wide spread of water laps over me with an enduring peace and excitement that feels like finding some precious rock in the earth, a sense of touching something that is most essentially me in a place where my past and my future intersect along the present. The present, that line of stress and connection and performance, the intense crashing now. Yet only earth and sky last forever, and the ocean joins them.

I hear the waters' song, feel the tides within the fluids of my body, hear the sea echoing my mothers' voices of survival from Elmina to Grenville to Harlem. I hear them resounding inside me from swish to boom—from the dark of the moon to fullness.

April 2, 1986
St. Croix, Virgin Islands

This is the year I spent spring beachcombing in St. Croix, awash with the trade winds and coconuts, sand and the sea. West Indian voices in the supermarket and Chase Bank, and the Caribbean flavors that have always meant home. Healing within a network of Black women who supplied everything from a steady stream of tender coconuts to spicy gossip to sunshine to fresh parrot fish to advice on how to cool out from academic burnout to a place where I can remember how the earth feels at 6:30 in the morning under a tropical crescent moon working in the still-cool garden—a loving context within which I fit and thrive.

I have been invited to take part in a conference on Caribbean women, "The Ties That Bind." At first I didn't think I'd have the energy to do it, but the whole experience has been a powerful and nourishing reminder of how good it feels to be doing my work where I'm convinced it matters the most, among the women—my sisters—who I most want to reach. It feels like I'm talking to Helen, my sister, and Carmen, my cousin, with all the attendant frustrations and joys rolled up together. It's always like this when you're trying to get people you love mightily to hear and use the ways in which you all are totally different, knowing they are the most difficult to reach. But it is the ways in which you are the same that make it possible to communicate at all.

The conference was organized by Gloria and the other three Sojourner Sisters, and it's an incredible accomplishment for four Black women with full-time jobs elsewhere to have pulled together such an ambitious enterprise. They orchestrated the entire event, bringing together presenters from ten different countries, feeding and housing us royally, as well as organizing four days of historical, cultural, and political presentations and workshops that were enjoyable and provocative for the more than 200 women who attended.

Johnnetta Cole's moving presentation of the Cuban revolution and its meaning in the lives of Caribbean women; Merle Hodge's incisive analysis of the sexism in calypsos; Dessima Williams, former ambassador from Grenada to the Organization of American States, proud and beautiful, recalling Maurice Bishop and Grenadian liberation with tears in her eyes.

In addition to being a tremendous high, these days are such a thrilling example to me of the real power of a small group of Black women of the diaspora in action. Four community women, meeting after work for almost a year, dreamed,

planned, financed, and executed this conference without insti-
tutional assistance. It has been an outstanding success, so much
information and affirmation for those of us who participated as
well as for those of us who attended.

It was a very centering experience for me, an ideal place for
me to step out again, and I was so proud to be a part of it, and to
speak and read my work as a Caribbean woman.

April 5, 1986
St. Croix
Yesterday was the eighteenth anniversary of Martin Luther
King's murder. Carnegie Hall, Duke Ellington, the Tougaloo
Choir. Their young Black voices tear in my blood to this day.
What the world needs now is love ... There was still a space left
for hope then, but the shore was fading fast. I wonder where all
those kids from Tougaloo are now who stood so brave and tear-
ful and together in their aloneness. I wonder how each of their
lives is being influenced/formed/informed by the emotions and
events upon that stage of Carnegie Hall that night King died. I
wonder if I will ever hear from any one of them again.

April 20, 1986
St. Croix
Blanchie's birthday. When Blanche had her mastectomy last
year, it was the first time that I had to face, in a woman I loved,
feelings and fears I had faced within my own self, but never
dealt with externally. Now I had to speak to these feelings in
some way that was meaningful and urgent in the name of my
love. Somehow I had known for the past eight years that some-
day it would be this way, that personal salvation of whatever
kind is never *just* personal.

I talked with Blanchie today over the phone about this feeling I have that I must rally everything I know, made alive and immediate with the fire of what is.

I have always been haunted by the fear of not being able to reach the women I am closest to, of not being able to make available to the women I love most dearly what I can make available to so many others. The women in my family, my closest friends. If what I know to be true cannot be of use to them, can it ever have been said to be true at all? On the other hand, that lays a terrible burden on all of us concerned, doesn't it?

It is a matter of learning languages, or of learning to use them with precision to do what needs to be done with them, and it is the Blanchie in myself to whom I need to speak with such urgency. It's one of the great things friends are for each other when you've been very close for a long time.

And of course cancer is political—look at how many of our comrades have died of it during the last ten years! As warriors, our job is to actively and consciously survive it for as long as possible, remembering that in order to win, the aggressor must conquer, but the resisters need only survive. Our battle is to define survival in ways that are acceptable and nourishing to us, meaning with substance and style. Substance. Our work. Style. True to our selves.

What would it be like to be living in a place where the pursuit of definition within this crucial part of our lives was not circumscribed and fractionalized by the economics of disease in america? Here the first consideration concerning cancer is not what does this mean in my living, but how much is this going to cost?

April 22, 1986
St. Croix
I got a letter from Ellen Kuzwayo this morning. Her sister in Botswana has died. I wish I were in Soweto to put my arms around her and rest her head on my shoulder. She sounds so strong and sanguine in her unshakable faith, yet so much alone. In the fabric of horrors that she and the other women live through daily in South Africa, this loss takes its place among so many others, at the same time particular and poignant.

May 8, 1986
New York City
Tomorrow belongs to those of us who conceive of it as belonging to everyone, who lend the best of ourselves to it, and with joy.

It takes all of my selves, working together, to integrate what I learn of women of Color around the world into my consciousness and work. It takes all of my selves working together to effectively focus attention and action against the holocaust progressing in South Africa and the South Bronx and Black schools across this nation, not to speak of the streets. Laying myself on the line. It takes all of my selves working together to fight this death inside me. Every one of these battles generates energies useful in the others.

I am on the cusp of change, and the curve is shifting fast.

In the bleakest days I am kept afloat, maintained, empowered, by the positive energies of so many women who carry the breath of my loving like firelight in their strong hair.

May 23, 1986
New York City
I spoke with Andrea in New Orleans this morning. She and Diana are helping to organize a Black Women's Book Fair.

Despite its size, there is not one feminist bookstore in the whole city. She's very excited about the project, and it was a real charge talking to her about it. There are so many young Black women across this country stepping out wherever they may be and making themselves felt within their communities in very real ways. These women make the early silence and the doubts and the wear and tear of it all worth it. I feel like they are my inheritors, and sometimes I breathe a sigh of relief that they exist, that I don't have to do it all.

It's a two-way street, and even I don't always realize it. Like the little sister from AA who stood up at my poetry reading last week and talked about how much courage I'd given her, and I was quaking in my boots because when she began I'd thought she was about to lay a heavy cancer rap on me in public, and I just wasn't quite ready for that yet. I feel very humbled behind that little episode. I want to acknowledge all those intricate connections between us by which we sustain and empower each other.

June 20, 1986
Bonnieux, France
How incredibly rich to be here in the south of France with the Zamani Soweto Sisters from South Africa. Gloria and I became acquainted with them through Ellen Kuzwayo and our fund-raising work with the Sisters in Support of Sisters in South Africa. They are one of the groups we help support through contributions. I'm only sorry that Ellen couldn't be here also, but at least I had a chance to share time and space with her in London on June 16, the anniversary of the Soweto uprising.

I learn tremendous courage from these women, from their laughter and their tears, from their grace under constant adversity, from their joy in living which is one of their most potent weapons, from the deft power of their large, overworked bodies and their dancing, swollen feet. In this brief respite for us all made possible by Betty Wolpert's kindness, these women have taught me so much courage and perspective.

June 21, 1986
Bonnieux

Sweet Solstice, and again the goddess smiles upon me. I am sitting in the stone-ringed yard of Les Quelles, a beautiful old reclaimed silk factory, now a villa. Gloria and the women of the Zamani Soweto Sisters surround me, all of us brilliant and subtle under the spreading flowers of a lime-tea tree. It looks and feels like what I've always imagined the women's compound in some African village to have been, once. Some of us drink tea, some are sewing, sweeping the dirt ground of the yard, hanging out clothes in the sunlight at the edge of the enclosure, washing, combing each other's hair. Acacia blossoms perfume the noon air as Vivian tells the stories behind the tears in her glowing amber eyes.

The young students who do not ask their parents' permission to run in the streets and die. The wealthy Black undertaker who lends his funeral hearses to the police to transport the bodies of the slain children.

The three little children who saw a heavy-armored Casspir barreling down the road in Dube and ran to hide behind the silk-cotton tree at the edge of the yard, too young to know that they could be seen as the tank rolled down the road. The blond policeman leaning out from the side of the tank to fire behind the tree at the little ones as they hid, reaching back over his shoulder to fire again as the vehicle rolled along, just to make sure the babies were all dead.

She tells of the mothers in her street who stay home from

work risking deportation to the barrenness of an alien "home-land," trudging from police station to police station all over Soweto asking, "Are my children here? Please sirs, this is her picture this is his school name he is nine years of age are my children here?" Her son leaving detention dragging his heels forever, achilles tendons torn and festering from untreated police dog bites.

Ruth, majestic and proud as Mujaji, ancient rain queen of the Lovedu. "I write my thoughts down on little scraps of paper," she says, talking about where the ideas come from for her intricate quilts. "And sometimes I pull them all out and read them and then I say no, that's not it at all and I throw them right away. But other times I smooth them out and save them for the quilts. I would like to keep a whole book of these stories from my life, but then a quilt is like a book of many stories done up together, and many people can read it all at the same time."

Gentle, strong, beautiful—the women of Soweto imprint their faces and their courage upon me. They enhance this French air, a cloud of soap and cosmetics and the lightest hint of hair cream. The knowledge of struggle never distant. Womanli-ness pervades this space.

Thembi, called Alice, flames under her taut sweetness, walking a dangerously narrow path too close to the swamp where there are bright lights flashing like stars just below the murky surface in harmony with the voices of astonished frogs in the green night. She begs me to release her from the pain of not doing enough for our own, of not making our daughters into ourselves. She tells me to dream upon all of their stories and write them a poem.

Petal, whose eyes are often too quiet as she moves about, short, solid, and graceful. We discuss love, comparing tales, and her eyes flash, amused and aglow. Other times they are wary, filled with distrust and grieving. Petal, who bore seven children and only two live. Who was tortured for weeks by the South African police. Who was helped by the International Hospital for Torture Victims in Switzerland.

Sula, wry and generous, knows how to get any question answered with a gentle inescapable persistence. Sometimes she drinks a lot. Her first husband broke her heart, but she quickly married again. "The missionaries lied to us so much about our bodies," she said, indignantly, "telling us they were dirty and we had to cover them up, and look now who is running about in bikinis on the Riviera, or naked and topless! I had a friend . . ." and she starts another story, like one most of these women tell, of a special woman friend who loved her past explaining.

Sweet-faced Emily tells of the militant young comrades in Soweto, their defiance of the old ways, carrying their determination for change into the streets. She demonstrates for us a spirited and high-stepping rendition of their rousing machine-gun dance. She does not like to listen to the other women singing hymns. Emily, who loved her best friend so much she still cannot listen to the records they once enjoyed together, and it is five years already since her friend died.

Linda of the hypnotic eyes who was questioned once by the South African police every single day for an entire month. About Zamani Soweto Sisters and subversive activities, such as a tiny ANC flag stitched on the little dead boy's pocket in the corner of a funeral procession quilt. "The quilts tell stories from our own lives. We did not know it was forbidden to sew the truth, but we will caution the women never to stitch such a thing again. No, thank you, I do not wish to take a cup of tea with you." I can hear her grave dignity speaking. She finishes the tale with a satisfied laugh.

Linda has a nineteen-year-old daughter. The women joke

and offer us their daughters to introduce to our sons and nephews in america. No one offers us their sons for our daughters.

Mariah lives next door to a famous woman writer in Soweto and offers to carry a letter to her from Kitchen Table: Women of Color Press. Posted mail from abroad so often does not reach its destination in Soweto. Round, quick, and with a brilliant smile, Mariah sits near the top of the executive board of Zamani. There is a presence about her of a successful African market woman, sharp, pleasant, outgoing, and awake to every opportunity.

Sofia keeps the books. She is quietly watchful and speaks with that soft humor that is shared by many of the women. She lives and sews alone now that her children are grown and gone away. She likes the way Gloria does her hair, and they discuss different hair preparations. Her eyes are encouraging and attentive as she sits and sews with tiny, rhythmical stitches.

Vibrant young Etta of the beautiful body dances excitement in our frequent spontaneous dancing. She is also learning to run the film cameras. Etta is always laughing and full of frolic, and some of the older women watch her and shake their heads with that particular Black women's look. But mostly they laugh back, because Etta's gaiety is so infectious. Her face turns serious as she discusses what she wants to do with her life back home.

Helen is another one of the young ones, as they are called by everyone else. Their relationship to the other women is clearly one of respect, almost like daughters-in-law. And this is in addition to the warmth and mutual esteem evident between all the women. Helen already moves in a dignified and considered way, but she has twinkling and mischievous eyes and tells me confidentially that she is the naughtiest one of all.

Rita, the last of the young ones, is quiet and small and rather proper. All the "mas" like her a lot, and smile approvingly at her. She is always helpful and soft-voiced, and really enjoys singing religious songs.

Bembe, light-skinned and small-boned, cleans and irons all day and sometimes at night when she is disturbed about something, like their imminent trip home. She is Zulu, like Etta, and loves to dance. Butterfly marks across her cheeks suggest she has lacked vitamins for a long time.

Hannah sings a spirited and humorous song about marriage being a stamping out of a woman's freedom, just like her signature in the marriage register is a stamping out of her own name as written in the book of life. All the other women join in the high-spirited chorus with much laughter. This is one of their favorite songs. Hannah talks about mothers-in-law, and how sometimes when they finally get to have their own way, they take it out on their sons' wives. And by tradition, the daughters-in-law must remain meek and helpful, blowing their lungs out firing the wood braziers and coal stoves for the rest of the family every morning. She tells of her own young self rising at 4:00 a.m., even on the morning after her wedding night, lighting the fire to fix her father-in-law his coffee. But she not only eventually stopped this, she even joined her daughter once in punching out her daughter's philandering husband, caught in the act in his wife's bed.

Mary, the oldest woman in the group, is called Number One. Witty, wise, and soft-spoken, she says love and concern came to her very late in life, once she started to work with Zamani. She is very grateful for the existence of the group, a sentiment that is often expressed by many of the other women in various ways. When we part she kisses me on my lips. "I love you, my sister," she says.

Wassa, round-cheeked and matter-of-fact, talks of her fear of reentry into Johannesburg. "But at least we will be all together," she says, "so if something happens to one of us the others can tell her people." I remember Ellen talking of the horror of hitting Jo'burg alone, and how you never know what the South African police might be planning for you at the airport, nor why.

The night before we part we swim in the pool beneath the sweet evening of the grapevines. "We are naked here in this pool now," Wassa says softly, "and we will be naked when we go back home." We told the women we would carry them in our hearts until we were together again. Everyone is anxious to go back home, despite the fear, despite the uncertainty, despite the dangers.

There is work to be done.

August 12, 1986
New York City
Wonderful news! My liver scan shows both tumors slightly diminished. It feels good to be getting on with my life. I feel vindicated without ever becoming complacent—this is only one victory of a long battle in which I've got to expect to win some and lose some. But it does put a different perspective upon things to know that pain can be a sign of a disintegrating tumor. Of course, my oncologist is surprised and puzzled. He admits he doesn't understand what is happening, but it is a mark of his good spirit that he is genuinely pleased for me, nonetheless. I'm very pleased for me, too.

A good autumn coming, if I remember to take it easily. I have interesting classes, and SISSA is planning a benefit this fall around the quilt Gloria and I brought back from the Zamani Soweto Sisters in europe. I'll be doing another benefit for Kitchen Table in Boston. That feels real good. It will be six years next month since the vision of KTP became a reality through the hard work of Barbara [Smith] and Cherrie [Moraga] and Myrna and the others.

August 15, 1986
New York City
Women of Color in struggle all over the world, our separate-
ness, our connectedness, so many more options for survival.
Whatever I call them, I know them for sister, mother, daughter,
voice and teacher, inheritor of fire. Alice of Soweto cursing the
mission songs: "We have our own political songs now for the
young people to sing—no more damn forgiveness!" Her voice
is almost hysterically alone in the shocked silence of the other
hymn-singing women.

Katerina stands in the Berlin hall, two hours into the dis-
cussion that follows the poetry reading by her and other Afro-
German women. "I have had enough," she says, "and yes, you
may need to continue to air your feelings of racism because for
you they are a new discovery here tonight. But I have known
them and lived with them all of my life and tonight it is now
time for me to go home." And she walks down the aisle and
out, straight and beautiful, with that fine and familiar Black
woman's audacity in the face of a totally unsupported situation.

Rangitunoa, Maori tribal woman, standing to speak in her
people's sacred place, the *marae*. Women have not spoken here
before because they have not known the ancient language. In
the old days, women did not speak in the *marae* at all. Now this
young woman who loves women stands to speak in the tongue
of her people, eloquently alone and suspect in her elders' eyes.

Dinah, Aboriginal woman come down from the hot north
hills of the outback, traveling by bus three days from mission to
mission to meet with the writing women of Melbourne, because
she had heard of this conference and she wishes to bring her
stories to them.

The stern, shy Samoan women in Auckland, plush and
mighty, organizing study groups for their teenaged kin,

holding evening classes for them in how to understand the *Pakahas* (whites).

The Aboriginal women reclaiming the famous Ayers Rock as *Ulluru*, a place of women's Dreaming.

The women of the South Pacific islands demanding their peoples' land rights, rejecting the european and american nuclear madness that is devastating their islands.

Brown people filling the streets of downtown Auckland, marching in support of a Nuclear Free and Independent Pacific. It could almost be Washington, D.C.!

Black children sitting down in the middle of metropolitan Melbourne to celebrate Koori Day, the black, red, and yellow flag of Pacific liberation and revolution snapping in the sun. "What do we want? LAND RIGHTS! When do we want them? NOW!!" Banners ringing the shopping mall in black, red, and yellow: PAY THE RENT!

Merle, fierce and shining, a Caribbean woman writer calmly analyzing the sexism behind the lyrics of beloved calypsos.

The Black South African seamstresses telling their multifaceted stories of survival, their soft voices filled with what Gloria calls a revolutionary patience.

Black women taking care of business all over the world.

September 21, 1986
New York City
The Autumn Equinox, a time of balancing. Nudie died of lung cancer today in Puerto Rico. Frances and I had just come back from a beautiful weekend in Shelter Island, and as we walked in the phone was ringing and it was Yoli. I feel that same sadness and fury as when I heard Hyllus Maris had died in Melbourne last month. Some of us refuse to have anything to do with other people who have cancer, reluctant to invite another

sorrow, as if any reflection of our own battle either lessens our power or makes it too realistic to be borne. Others of us fashion a connection of support, but sometimes that connection is not solid enough and invites another grief. I felt I had a special pact with Hyllus and with Nudie. As if we had promised each other we would make it, but nobody does, and they didn't, and I won't either.

But magical thinking doesn't work. I'm so glad Nudie had a chance to go back to Puerto Rico, which is where she always wanted to end up her time.

Making it really means doing it our way for as long as possible, same as crossing a busy avenue or telling unpleasant truths. But even though it's childish and useless, I'm still angry with both of them for dying.

That's probably how some of my friends feel about me right now, the ones who can't look me in the eye when they ask how I'm doing, even though I'm very much alive and kicking.

It's nine years ago today I had my first breast biopsy. Which was outstandingly and conclusively negative. So much for biopsies.

September 27, 1986
New York City
I hope when I reread this journal later there will be more here than simply a record of who died in what month and how their passing touched me. Maybe at least how I can use that knowledge to move beyond the moments of terror. I much prefer to think about how I'd want to die—given that I don't want to die at all but will certainly have to—rather than just fall into death any old way, by default, according to somebody else's rules. It's not like you get a second chance to die the way you want to die.

Sometimes I have the eeriest feeling that I'm living some macabre soap opera. And *too besides*, it's being recorded in vivid living color. If so, I hope it'll be useful someday for something, if only for some other Black sister's afternoon entertainment when her real life gets to be too much. It'll sure beat *As the World Turns*. At least there will be real Black people in this one, and maybe if I'm lucky, I'll get to drag the story on interminably for twenty or thirty years like the TV soaps, until the writer dies of old age or the audience loses interest—which is another way of saying they no longer need to discharge the tensions in their lives that lie behind that particular story.

November 6, 1986
New York City
Black mother goddess, salt dragon of chaos, Seboulisa, Mawu. Attend me, hold me in your muscular flowering arms, protect me from throwing any part of myself away.

Women who have asked me to set these stories down are asking me for my air to breathe, to use in their future, are courting me back to my life as a warrior. Some offer me their bodies, some their enduring patience, some a separate fire, and still others, only a naked need whose face is all too familiar. It is the need to give voice to the complexities of living with cancer, outside of the tissue-thin assurance that they "got it all," or that the changes we have wrought in our lives will insure that cancer never reoccurs. And it is a need to give voice to living with cancer outside of that numbing acceptance of death as a resignation waiting after fury and before despair.

There is nothing I cannot use somehow in my living and my work, even if I would never have chosen it on my own, even if I am livid with fury at having to choose. Not only did nobody ever say it would be easy, nobody ever said what faces the challenges would wear. The point is to do as much as I can of what I came to do before they nickel and dime me to death.

Racism. Cancer. In both cases, to win the aggressor must conquer, but the resisters need only survive. How do I define that survival and on whose terms?

So I feel a sense of triumph as I pick up my pen and say yes I am going to write again from the world of cancer and with a different perspective—that of living with cancer in an intimate daily relationship. Yes, I'm going to say plainly, six years after my mastectomy, in spite of drastically altered patterns of eating and living, and in spite of my self-conscious living and increased self-empowerment, and in spite of my deepening commitment to using myself in the service of what I believe, and in spite of all my positive expectations to the contrary, I have been diagnosed as having cancer of the liver, metastasized from breast cancer.

This fact does not make my last six years of work any less vital or important or necessary. The accuracy of that diagnosis has become less important than how I use the life I have.

November 8, 1986
New York City

If I am to put this all down in a way that is useful, I should start with the beginning of the story.

Sizable tumor in the right lobe of the liver, the doctors said. Lots of blood vessels in it means it's most likely malignant. Let's cut you open right now and see what we can do about it. Wait a minute, I said. I need to feel this thing out and see what's going on inside myself first, I said, needing some time to absorb the shock, time to assay the situation and not act out of panic. Not one of them said, I can respect that, but don't take too long about it.

Instead, that simple claim to my body's own processes elicited such an attack response from a reputable Specialist In Liver Tumors that my deepest—if not necessarily most useful—suspicions were totally aroused.

What that doctor could have said to me that I would have heard was, "You have a serious condition going on in your body and whatever you do about it you must not ignore it or delay deciding how you are going to deal with it because it will not go away no matter what you think it is." Acknowledging my responsibility for my own body. Instead, what he said to me was, "If you do not do exactly what I tell you to do right now without questions you are going to die a horrible death." In exactly those words.

I felt the battle lines being drawn up within my own body.

I saw this specialist in liver tumors at a leading cancer hospital in New York City, where I had been referred as an outpatient by my own doctor.

The first people who interviewed me in white coats from behind a computer were only interested in my health-care benefits and proposed method of payment. Those crucial facts determined what kind of plastic ID card I would be given, and without a plastic ID card, no one at all was allowed upstairs to see any doctor, as I was told by the uniformed, pistoled guards at all the stairwells.

From the moment I was ushered into the doctor's office and he saw my x-rays, he proceeded to infantilize me with an obviously well-practiced technique. When I told him I was having second thoughts about a liver biopsy, he glanced at my chart. Racism and sexism joined hands across his table as he saw I taught at a university. "Well, you look like an *intelligent girl*," he said, staring at my one breast all the time he was speaking. "Not to have this biopsy immediately is like sticking your head in the sand." Then he went on to say that he would not be responsible when I wound up one day screaming in agony in the corner of his office!

I asked this specialist in liver tumors about the dangers of a liver biopsy spreading an existing malignancy, or even encouraging it in a borderline tumor. He dismissed my concerns with a wave of his hand, saying, instead of answering, that I really did not have any other sensible choice.

I would like to think that this doctor was sincerely motivated by a desire for me to seek what he truly believed to be the only remedy for my sickening body, but my faith in that scenario is considerably diminished by his $250 consultation fee and his subsequent medical report to my own doctor containing numerous supposedly clinical observations of *obese abdomen and remaining pendulous breast*.

In any event, I can thank him for the fierce shard lancing through my terror that shrieked there must be some other way, this doesn't feel right to me. If this is cancer and they cut me open to find out, what is stopping that intrusive action from spreading the cancer, or turning a questionable mass into an active malignancy? All I was asking for was the reassurance of a realistic answer to my real questions, and that was not forthcoming. I made up my mind that if I was going to die in agony on somebody's office floor, it certainly wasn't going to be his! I needed information, and pored over books on the liver in Barnes & Noble's medical textbook section on Fifth Avenue for hours. I learned, among other things, that the liver is the largest, most complex, and most generous organ in the human body. But that did not help me very much.

In this period of physical weakness and psychic turmoil, I

found myself going through an intricate inventory of rage. First of all at my breast surgeon—had he perhaps done something wrong? How could such a small breast tumor have metastasized? Hadn't he assured me he'd gotten it all, and what was this now anyway about micro-metastases? Could this tumor in my liver have been seeded at the same time as my breast cancer? There were so many unanswered questions, and too much that I just did not understand.

But my worst rage was the rage at myself. For a brief time I felt like a total failure. What had I been busting my ass doing these past six years if it wasn't living and loving and working to my utmost potential? And wasn't that all a guarantee supposed to keep exactly this kind of thing from ever happening again? So what had I done wrong and what was I going to have to pay for it and WHY ME?

But finally a little voice inside me said sharply, "Now really, is there any other way you would have preferred living the past six years that would have been more satisfying? And be that as it may, *should or shouldn't* isn't even the question. How do you want to live the rest of your life from now on and what are you going to do about it?" Time's a-wasting!

Gradually, in those hours in the stacks of Barnes & Noble, I felt myself shifting into another gear. My resolve strengthened as my panic lessened. Deep breathing, regularly. I'm not going to let them cut into my body again until I'm convinced there is no other alternative. And this time, the burden of proof rests with the doctors because their record of success with liver cancer is not so good that it would make me jump at a surgical solution. And scare tactics are not going to work. I have been scared now for six years and that hasn't stopped me. I've given myself plenty of practice in doing whatever I need to do, scared or not, so scare tactics are just not going to work. Or I hoped they were not going to work. At any rate, thank the goddess, they were not working yet. One step at a time.

But some of my nightmares were pure hell, and I started having trouble sleeping.

In writing this I have discovered how important some things are that I thought were unimportant. I discovered this by the high price they exact for scrutiny. At first I did not want to look again at how I slowly came to terms with my own mortality on a level deeper than before, nor with the inevitable strength that gave me as I started to get on with my life in actual time. Medical textbooks on the liver were fine, but there were appointments to be kept, and bills to pay, and decisions about my upcoming trip to europe to be made. And what do I say to my children? Honesty has always been the bottom line between us, but did I really need them going through this with me during their final difficult years at college? On the other hand, how could I shut them out of this most important decision of my life?

I made a visit to my breast surgeon, a doctor with whom I have always been able to talk frankly, and it was from him that I got my first trustworthy and objective sense of timing. It was from him that I learned that the conventional forms of treatment for liver metastases made little more than one year's difference in the survival rate. I heard my old friend Clem's voice coming back to me through the dimness of thirty years: "I see you coming here trying to make sense where there is no sense. Try just living in it. Respond, alter, see what happens." I thought of the African way of perceiving life, as experience to be lived rather than as problem to be solved.

Homeopathic medicine calls cancer the cold disease. I understand that down to my bones that quake sometimes in their need for heat, for the sun, even for just a hot bath. Part of the way in which I am saving my own life is to refuse to submit my body to cold whenever possible.

In general, I fight hard to keep my treatment scene together in some coherent and serviceable way, integrated into my daily living and absolute. Forgetting is no excuse. It's as simple as one missed shot could make the difference between a quiescent malignancy and one that is growing again. This not only keeps me in an intimate, positive relationship to my own health, but it also underlines the fact that I have the responsibility for attending my own health. I cannot simply hand over that responsibility to anybody else.

Which does not mean I give in to the belief, arrogant or naive, that I know everything I need to know in order to make informed decisions about my body. But attending my own health, gaining enough information to help me understand and participate in the decisions made about my body by people who know more medicine than I do, are all crucial strategies in my battle for living. They also provide me with important prototypes for doing battle in all other arenas of my life.

Battling racism and battling heterosexism and battling apartheid share the same urgency inside me as battling cancer. None of these struggles are ever easy, and even the smallest victory is never to be taken for granted. Each victory must be applauded, because it is so easy not to battle at all, to just accept and call that acceptance inevitable.

And all power is relative. Recognizing the existence as well as the limitations of my own power, and accepting the responsibility for using it in my own behalf, involve me in direct and daily actions that preclude denial as a possible refuge. Simone de Beauvoir's words echo in my head: "It is in the recognition of the genuine conditions of our lives that we gain the strength to act and our motivation for change."

November 10, 1986
New York City

Building into my living—without succumbing to it—an awareness of this reality of my life, that I have a condition within my body of which I will eventually die, comes in waves, like a rising tide. It exists side by side with another force inside me that says no you don't, not you, and the x-rays are wrong and the tests are wrong and the doctors are wrong.

There is a different kind of energy inherent within each one of these feelings, and I try to reconcile and use these different energies whenever I need them. The energy generated by the first awareness serves to urge me always to get on with living my life and doing my work with an intensity and purpose of the urgent now. Throw the toys overboard, we're headed into rougher waters.

The energies generated by the second force fuel a feisty determination to continue doing what I am doing forever. The tensions created inside me by the contradictions is another source of energy and learning. I have always known I learn my most lasting lessons about difference by closely attending the ways in which the differences inside me lie down together.

November 11, 1986
New York City

I keep observing how other people die, comparing, learning, critiquing the process inside of me, matching it up to how I would like to do it. And I think about this scrutiny of myself in the context of its usefulness to other Black women living with cancer, born and unborn.

I have a privileged life or else I would be dead by now. It is two and a half years since the first tumor in my liver was discovered. When I needed to know, there was no one around to tell me that there were alternatives to turning myself over to doctors who are terrified of not knowing everything. There was no one around to remind me that I have a right to decide what happens to my own body, not because I know more than anybody else, but simply because it is my body. And I have a right to acquire the information that can help me make those crucial decisions.

It was an accident of circumstance that brought me to Germany at a critical moment in my health, and another which introduced me to one holistic/homeopathic approach to the treatment of certain cancers. Not all homeopathic alternatives work for every patient. Time is a crucial element in the treatment of cancer, and I had to decide which chances I would take, and why.

I think of what this means to other Black women living with cancer, to all women in general. Most of all I think of how important it is for us to share with each other the powers buried within the breaking of silence about our bodies and our health, even though we have been schooled to be secret and stoical about pain and disease. But that stoicism and silence does not serve us nor our communities, only the forces of things as they are.

November 12, 1986
New York City
When I write my own Book of the Dead, my own Book of Life, I want to celebrate being alive to do it even while I acknowledge the painful savor uncertainty lends to my living. I use the energy of dreams that are now impossible, not totally believing in them nor their power to become real, but recognizing them as

templates for a future within which my labors can play a part. I am freer to choose what I will devote my energies toward and what I will leave for another lifetime, thanking the goddess for the strength to perceive that I can choose, despite obstacles.

So when I do a SISA reading to raise funds for the women's collectives in Soweto, or to raise money for Kitchen Table: Women of Color Press, I am choosing to use myself for things in which I passionately believe. When I speak to rally support in the urgent war against apartheid in South Africa and the racial slaughter that is even now spreading across the U.S., when I demand justice in the police shotgun killing of a Black grandmother and lynchings in northern California and in Central Park in New York City, I am making a choice of how I wish to use my power. This work gives me a tremendous amount of energy back in satisfaction and in belief, as well as in a vision of how I want this earth to be for the people who come after me.

When I work with young poets who are reaching for the power of their poetry within themselves and the lives they choose to live, I feel I am working to capacity, and this gives me deep joy, a reservoir of strength I draw upon for the next venture. Right now. This makes it far less important that it will not be forever. It never was.

The energies I gain from my work help me neutralize those implanted forces of negativity and self-destructiveness that is white america's way of making sure I keep whatever is powerful and creative within me unavailable, ineffective, and nonthreatening.

But there is a terrible clarity that comes from living with cancer that can be empowering if we do not turn aside from it. What more can they do to me? My time is limited, and this is so for each one of us. So how will the opposition reward me for my silences? For the pretense that this is in fact the best of all possible worlds? What will they give me for lying? A lifelong Safe Conduct Pass for everyone I love? Another lifetime for me? The end to racism? Sexism? Homophobia? Cruelty? The common cold?

November 13, 1986
New York City
I do not find it useful any longer to speculate upon cancer as a political weapon. But I'm not being paranoid when I say my cancer is as political as if some CIA agent brushed past me in the A train on March 15, 1965, and air-injected me with a long-fused cancer virus. Or even if it is only that I stood in their wind to do my work and the billows flayed me. What possible choices do most of us have in the air we breathe and the water we must drink?

Sometimes we are blessed with being able to choose the time and the arena and the manner of our revolution, but more usually we must do battle wherever we are standing. It does not matter too much if it is in the radiation lab or a doctor's office or the telephone company, the streets, the welfare department, or the classroom. The real blessing is to be able to use whoever I am wherever I am, in concert with as many others as possible, or alone if needs be.

This is no longer a time of waiting. It is a time for the real work's urgencies. It is a time enhanced by an iron reclamation of what I call the burst of light—that inescapable knowledge, in the bone, of my own physical limitation. Metabolized and integrated into the fabric of my days, that knowledge makes the particulars of what is coming seem less important. When I speak of wanting as much good time as possible, I mean time over which I maintain some relative measure of control.

November 14, 1986
New York City

One reason I watch the death process so acutely is to rob it of some of its power over my consciousness. I have overcome my earlier need to ignore or turn away from films and books that deal with cancer or dying. It is ever so much more important now for me to fill the psyches of all the people I love and who love me with a sense of outrageous beauty and strength of purpose.

But it is also true that sometimes we cannot heal ourselves close to the very people from whom we draw strength and light, because they are also closest to the places and tastes and smells that go along with a pattern of living we are trying to rearrange. After my mastectomy, changing the ways I ate and struggled and slept and meditated also required that I change the external environment within which I was deciding what direction I would have to take.

I am on the cusp of change and the curve is shifting fast. If any of my decisions have been in error, I must stand—not prepared, for that is impossible—but open to dealing with the consequences of those errors.

Inside and outside, change is not easy nor quick, and I find myself always on guard against what is oversimplified, or merely cosmetic.

November 15, 1986
New York City

In my office at home I have created a space that is very special to me. It is simple and quiet, with beautiful things about, and a ray of sunlight cascading through a low window on the best of days. It is here that I write whenever I am home, and where I retreat to center myself, to rest and recharge at regular intervals. It is here that I do my morning visualizations and my eurhythmics.

It is a tiny alcove with an air mattress half-covered with bright pillows, and a low narrow table with a Nigerian tie-dye throw. Against one wall and central to this space is a painting by a young Guyanese woman called *The Yard*. It is a place of water and fire and flowers and trees, filled with Caribbean women and children working and playing and being.

When the sun lances through my small window and touches the painting, the yard comes alive. The red spirit who lives at the center of the painting flames. Children laugh, a woman nurses her baby, a little naked boy cuts the grass. One woman is building a fire outside for cooking; inside a house another woman is fixing a light. In a slat-house up the hill, windows are glowing under the red-tiled roof.

I keep company with the women of this place.

Yesterday, I sat in this space with a sharp Black woman, discussing the focus of a proposed piece for a Black women's magazine. We talked about whether it should be about the role of art and spirituality in Black women's lives, or about my survival struggles with current bouts of cancer.

As we talked, I gradually realized that both articles were grounded in the same place within me, and required the same focus. I require the nourishment of art and spirituality in my life, and they lend strength and insight to all the endeavors that give substance to my living. It is the bread of art and the water of my spiritual life that remind me always to reach for what is highest within my capacities and in my demands of myself and others. Not for what is perfect but for what is the best possible. And I orchestrate my daily anticancer campaign with an intensity intrinsic to who I am, the intensity of making a poem. It is the same intensity with which I experience poetry, a student's first breakthrough, the loving energy of women I do not even know, the posted photograph of a sunrise taken from my winter dawn window, the intensity of loving.

I revel in the beauty of the faces of Black women at labor and at rest. I make, demand, translate satisfactions out of every ray of sunlight, scrap of bright cloth, beautiful sound, delicious smell that comes my way, out of every sincere smile and good wish. They are discreet bits of ammunition in my arsenal against despair. They all contribute to the strengthening of my determination to persevere when the greyness overwhelms, or Reaganomics wears me down. They whisper to me of joy when the light is dim, when I falter, when another Black child is gunned down from behind in Crossroads or Newark or lynched from a tree in Memphis, and when the health orchestration gets boring or depressing or just plain too much.

November 16, 1986
New York City
For Black women, learning to consciously extend ourselves to each other and to call upon each other's strengths is a life-saving strategy. In the best of circumstances surrounding our lives, it requires an enormous amount of mutual, consistent support for us to be emotionally able to look straight into the face of the powers aligned against us and still do our work with joy.

It takes determination and practice.

Black women who survive have a head start in learning how to be open and self-protective at the same time. One secret is to ask as many people as possible for help, depending on all of them and on none of them at the same time. Some will help, others cannot. For the time being.

Another secret is to find some particular thing your soul craves for nourishment—a different religion, a quiet spot, a dance class—and satisfy it. That satisfaction does not have to be costly or difficult. Only a need that is recognized, articulated, and answered.

There is an important difference between openness and naiveté. Not everyone has good intentions nor means me well. I remind myself I do not need to change these people, only recognize who they are.

November 17, 1986
New York City

How has everyday living changed for me with the advent of a second cancer? I move through a terrible and invigorating savor of now—a visceral awareness of the passage of time, with its nightmare and its energy. No more long-term loans, extended payments, twenty-year plans. Pay my debts. Call the tickets in, the charges, the emotional IOUs. Now is the time, if ever, once and for all, to alter the patterns of isolation. Remember that nice lady down the street whose son you used to cross at the light and who was always saying, "Now if there's ever anything I can do for you, just let me know." Well, her boy's got strong muscles and the lawn needs mowing.

I am not ashamed to let my friends know I need their collective spirit—not to make me live forever, but rather to help me move through the life I have. But I refuse to spend the rest of that life mourning what I do not have.

If living as a poet—living on the front lines—has ever had meaning, it has meaning now. Living a self-conscious life, vulnerability as armor.

I spend time every day meditating upon my physical self in battle, visualizing the actual war going on inside my body. As I move through the other parts of each day, that battle often merges with particular external campaigns, both political and personal. The devastations of apartheid in South Africa and racial murder in Howard Beach feel as critical to me as cancer.

Among my other daily activities I incorporate brief periods of physical self-monitoring without hysteria. I attend the changes within my body, anointing myself with healing light. Sometimes I have to do it while sitting on the Staten Island Ferry on my way home, surrounded by snapping gum and dirty rubber boots, all of which I banish from my consciousness.

I am learning to reduce stress in my practical everyday living. It's nonsense, however, to believe that any Black woman who is living an informed life in america can possibly abolish stress totally from her life without becoming psychically deaf, mute, and blind. (*News item: Unidentified Black man found hanging from a tree in Central Park with hands and feet bound. New York City police call it a suicide.*) I am learning to balance stress with periods of rest and restoration.

I juggle the technologies of eastern medicine with the holistic approach of anthroposophy with the richness of my psychic life, beautifully and womanfully nourished by people I love and who love me. Balancing them all. Knowing over and over again how blessed I am in my life, my loves, my children; how blessed I am in being able to give myself to work in which I passionately believe. And yes, some days I wish to heaven to Mawu to Seboulisa to Tiamat daughter of chaos that it could all have been easier.

But I wake in an early morning to see the sun rise over the tenements of Brooklyn across the bay, fingering through the wintered arms of the raintree Frances and I planted as a thin stick seventeen years ago, and I cannot possibly imagine trading my life for anyone else's, no matter how near termination that life may be. Living fully—how long is not the point. How and why take total precedence.

November 18, 1986
New York City

Despair and isolation are my greatest internal enemies. I need to remember I am not alone, even when it feels that way. Now more than ever it is time to put my solitary ways behind me, even while protecting my solitude. "Help is on the way," Margareta said, her fingers moving over the Tarot deck in a farewell gesture.

I need to identify that help and use it whenever I can.

Five million people in the U.S.—or 2 percent of the population of this country—are actively living with cancer. If you apply that percentage to the Black community—where it is probably higher because of the rising incidence of cancers without a corresponding rise in the cure rate—if we take that percentage into the Black population of 22 million, then every single day there are at least half a million Black people in the U.S. shopping in supermarkets, catching subways, grooming mules, objecting in PTA meetings, standing in a welfare line, teaching Sunday school, walking in the streets at noon looking for work, scrubbing a kitchen floor, all carrying within our bodies the seeds of a destruction not of our own choosing. It is a destruction we can keep from defining our living for as long as possible, if not our dying. Each one of us must define for ourselves what substance and shape we wish to give the life we have left.

November 19, 1986
New York City

Evil never appears in its own face to bargain, nor does impotence, nor does despair. After all, who believes any more in the devil buying up souls, anyway? But I warn myself, don't even pretend not to say no, loudly and often, no matter how symbolically. Because the choices presented in our lives are never simple or fable-clear. Survival never presents itself as "do this particular thing precisely as directed and you will go on living. Don't do that and no question about it you will surely die." Despite what the doctor said, it just doesn't happen that way.

Probably in some ideal world we would be offered distinct choices, where we make our decisions from a clearly typed and annotated menu. But no life for any Black woman I know is that simple or that banal. There are as many crucial, untimed decisions to be made as there are dots in a newspaper photo of great contrast, and as we get close enough to examine them within their own terrain, the whole picture becomes distorted and obscure.

I do not think about my death as being imminent, but I live my days against a background noise of mortality and constant uncertainty.

Learning not to crumple before these uncertainties fuels my resolve to print myself upon the texture of each day fully rather than forever.

December 1, 1986
New York City
Cancer survivors are expected to be silent out of misguided concerns for others' feelings of guilt or despair, or out of a belief in the myth that there can be self-protection through secrecy. By and large, outside the radiation lab or the doctor's office, we are invisible to each other, and we begin to be invisible to ourselves. We begin to doubt whatever power we once knew we had, and once we doubt our power, we stop using it. We rob our comrades, our lovers, our friends, and our selves of ourselves.

I have periods of persistent and distracting visceral discomfort that are totally intrusive and energy-consuming. I say this rather than simply use the word *pain*, because there are too many gradations of effect and response that are not covered by that one word. Self-hypnosis seemed a workable possibility for maintaining some control over the processes going on inside my body. With trial and inquiry, I found a reliable person to train me in the techniques of self-hypnosis. It's certainly cheaper than codeine.

Self-hypnosis requires a concentration so intense I put myself into a waking trance. But we go into those states more often than we realize. Have you ever been wide awake on the subway and missed your station because you were thinking about something else? It's a question of recognizing this state and learning to use it to manipulate my consciousness of pain.

One of the worst things about intrusive pain is that it makes me feel impotent, unable to move against it and therefore against anything else, as if the pain swallows up all ability to act. Self-hypnosis has been useful to me not only for refocusing physical discomfort, it has also been useful to me in helping effect other bargains with my unconscious self. I've been able to use it to help me remember my dreams, raise a subnormal body temperature, and bring myself to complete a difficult article.

I respect the time I spend each day treating my body, and I consider it part of my political work. It is possible to have some conscious input into our physical processes—not expecting the impossible, but allowing for the unexpected—a kind of training in self-love and physical resistance.

December 7, 1986
New York City
I'm glad I don't have to turn away any more from movies about people dying of cancer. I no longer have to deny cancer as a reality in my life. As I wept over *Terms of Endearment* last night,

I also laughed. It's hard to believe I avoided this movie for over two years.

Yet while I was watching it, involved in the situation of a young mother dying of breast cancer, I was also very aware of that standard of living, taken for granted in the film, that made the expression of her tragedy possible. Her mother's maid and the manicured garden, the unremarked but very tangible money so evident through its effects. Daughter's philandering husband is an unsuccessful English professor, but they still live in a white-shingled house with trees, not in some rack-ass tenement on the Lower East Side or in Harlem for which they pay too much rent.

Her private room in Lincoln Memorial Hospital has her mama's Renoir on the wall. There are never any Black people at all visible in that hospital in Lincoln, Nebraska, not even in the background. Now this may not make her death scenes any less touching, but it did strengthen my resolve to talk about my experiences with cancer as a Black woman.

December 14, 1986
New York City
It is exactly one year since I went to Switzerland and found the air cold and still. Yet what I found at the Lukas Klinik has helped me save my life.

[Its manifestation is not only therapeutic. It is vital. Under-lining what is joyful and life-affirming in my living becomes crucial.

What have I had to leave behind? Old life habits, outgrown defenses put aside lest they siphon off energies to no useful purpose?

One of the hardest things to accept is learning to live within uncertainty and neither deny it nor hide behind it. Most of all, to listen to the messages of uncertainty without allowing them to immobilize me, nor keep me from the certainties of those truths in which I believe. I turn away from any need to justify the future—to live in what has not yet been. Believing, working for what has not yet been while living fully in the present now.

This is my life. Each hour is a possibility not to be banked. These days are not a preparation for living, some necessary but essentially extraneous divergence from the main course of my living. They are my life. The feeling of the bedsheet against my heels as I wake to the sound of crickets and bananaquits in Judith's Fancy. I am living my life every particular day no matter where I am, nor in what pursuit. It is the consciousness of this that gives a marvelous breadth to everything I do consciously. My most deeply held convictions and beliefs can be equally expressed in how I deal with chemotherapy as well as in how I scrutinize a poem. It's about trying to know who I am wherever I am. It's not as if I'm in struggle over here while someplace else, over there, real life is waiting for me to begin living it again.

I visualize daily winning the battles going on inside my body, and this is an important part of fighting for my life. In those visualizations, the cancer at times takes on the face and shape of my most implacable enemies, those I fight and resist most fiercely. Sometimes the wanton cells in my liver become Bull Connor and his police dogs completely smothered, rendered impotent in Birmingham, Alabama, by a mighty avalanche of young, determined Black marchers moving across him toward their future. P. W. Botha's bloated face of apartheid squashed into the earth beneath an onslaught of the slow rhythmic advance of furious Blackness. Black South African women moving through my blood destroying passbooks. Fireburn Mary sweeping over the Cruzan countryside, axe and torch in hand. Images from a Calypso singer:

The big black boot of freedom
Is mashing down your doorstep.

I train myself for triumph by knowing it is mine, no matter what. In fact, I am surrounded within my external living by ample examples of the struggle for life going on inside me. Visualizing the disease process inside my body in political images is not a quixotic dream. When I speak out against the cynical U.S. intervention in Central America, I am working to save my life in every sense. Government research grants to the National Cancer Institute were cut in 1986 by the exact amount illegally turned over to the contras in Nicaragua. One hundred and five million dollars. It gives yet another meaning to the personal as the political.

Cancer itself has an anonymous face. When we are visibly dying of cancer, it is sometimes easier to turn away from the particular experience into the sadness of loss, and when we are surviving, it is sometimes easier to deny that experience. But those of us who live our battles in the flesh must know ourselves as our strongest weapon in the most gallant struggle of our lives.

Living with cancer has forced me to consciously jettison the myth of omnipotence, of believing—or loosely asserting—that I can do anything, along with any dangerous illusion of immortality. Neither of these unscrutinized defenses is a solid base for either political activism or personal struggle. But in their place, another kind of power is growing, tempered and enduring, grounded within the realities of what I am in fact doing. An open-eyed assessment and appreciation of what I can and do accomplish, using who I am and who I most wish myself to be. To stretch as far as I can go and relish what is satisfying rather than what is sad. Building a strong and elegant pathway toward transition.

I work, I love, I rest, I see and learn. And I report. These are my givens. Not sureties, but a firm belief that whether or not living them with joy prolongs my life, it certainly enables me to pursue the objectives of that life with a deeper and more effective clarity.

August 1987
Carriacou, Grenada
Anguilla, British West Indies
St. Croix, Virgin Islands

Is Your Hair Still Political?

My first trip to Virgin Gorda earlier this year had been an enjoyable, relaxing time. After coping with the devastations of Hurricane Hugo, three friends and I decided to meet somewhere in the Caribbean for a Christmas vacation. From my personal and professional travels, Virgin Gorda seemed the ideal spot. And less than an hour's flight time from my home.

My friend, another Black woman from St. Croix, and I deplaned in Tortola to clear BVI [British Virgin Islands] immigration at the Beef Island Airport. I was happy to be a tourist for a change, looking forward to a wonderful holiday, post-hurricane problems left behind for a few days. The morning was brilliant and sunny, and in our bags was a frozen turkey, along with decorations for the rented house.

The Black woman in a smartly pressed uniform behind the Immigration Control desk was younger than I, with heavily processed hair flawlessly styled. I handed her my completed entry card. She looked up at me, took it with a smile, and said, "Who does your hair?"

My friend and I were the only passengers going on to Virgin Gorda. As a Black woman writer who travels widely, I have recently been asked that question many times. Thinking we were about to embark on one of those conversations about hairstyle Black women so often have in passing, on supermarket lines, buses, in laundromats, I told her I had done it myself. Upon her further questioning, I described how.

I was not at all prepared when, still smiling, she suddenly said, "Well, you can't come in here with your hair like that you know." And reaching over she stamped "no admittance" across my visitor's card.

"Oh, I didn't know," I said, "then I'll cover it," and I pulled out my headkerchief.

"That won't make any difference," she said. "The next plane back to St. Croix is 5:00 p.m. this evening." By this time my friend, who wears her hair in braided extensions, tried to come to my aid. "What's wrong with her hair," she asked, "and what about mine?"

"Yours is all right," she was told. "That's just a hairstyle."

"But mine is just a hairstyle too," I protested, still not believing this was happening to me. I had traveled freely all over the world; now, in a Caribbean country, a Black woman was telling me I could not enter her land because of how I wore my hair?

"There is a law on our books," she said. "You can't come in here looking LIKE THAT."

I touched my natural locks, of which I was so proud. A year ago I had decided to stop cutting my hair and to grow locks as a personal style statement, much the same as I had worn a natural afro for most of my adult life. I remembered an *Essence* magazine cover story in the early 80s that had inspired one of my most popular poems—*Is Your Hair Still Political?*

"You can't be serious," I said. "Then why didn't I know about this before? Where is it written in any of your tourist information that Black women are only allowed to wear our hair in certain styles in your country? And why do we have to?"

Her smile was gone by now.

"It's been a law for over five years," she snapped. And I realized she was very serious when I saw our bags being taken off the plane, and it preparing to go on without us.

"But how was I supposed to know that?" I protested, visions of our holiday feast defrosting on the tarmac, our friends from New York wondering where we were, our hostess at the airport waiting in vain to drive us to our rented house by the sea.

"I've read I can't bring drugs into the British Virgin Islands. I've read I can't seek employment in the British Virgin Islands. I've read about everything else I can't do in the British Virgin Islands, but how are Black tourists supposed to know we can't wear locks if we visit the British Virgin Islands? Or don't you want Black tourists?"

By now I was outraged. Even with the hot sun outside and the dark face before me, I was confused for a moment as to where I was. Nazi Germany? Fascist Spain? Racist South Africa? One of those places where for so many decades white people had excluded Black people because of how they LOOKED? But no, it was a Black woman, in the Caribbean, telling me I wasn't acceptable as a tourist in her country—not because of what I do, not even because of who I am, but because of how I wear my hair. I felt chilled to the bone.

By this time the young white pilot had come in to see why the flight was being delayed. "What do you mean, because of her HAIR?" Finally an immigration supervisor came, asking me to fill out another entry card.

"Why can't I go on to Virgin Gorda," I began. "I've been there before. And what's wrong with my hair? It's not unhealthy, it's not unsanitary, it's not immoral, and it certainly is not unnatural!"

The supervisor looked at my well-groomed ear-length locks. "Are you a Rasta?" he asked. And then it finally dawned on me what this was all about.

He didn't ask me if I was a murderer. He didn't ask me if I was a drug dealer, or a racist, or if I was a member of the Ku Klux Klan. Instead, he asked me if I was a follower of the Rastafarian religion.

Some see locks and they see revolution. Because Rastafarians smoke marijuana as a religious rite, some see locks and automatically see drug peddlers. But the people who are pushing drugs throughout the Caribbean do not wear locks; they wear three-piece suits, carry attaché cases and diplomatic pouches, and usually have no trouble at all passing through Immigration.

I stared at this earnest young Black man for a moment. Suddenly my hair became very political. Waves of horror washed over me. How many forms of religious persecution are we now going to visit upon each other as Black people in the name of our public safety? And suppose I was a Rastafarian? What then? Why did that automatically mean I could not vacation in Virgin Gorda? Did it make my tourist dollars unusable?

What if he had asked me if I were a Jew? A Quaker? A Protestant? A Catholic? What have we learned from the bloody pages of history and are we really doomed to repeat these mistakes?

There was an ache in my heart. I wanted to say, "What does it matter if I am a Rasta or not?" But I saw our bags sitting out in the sun, and the pilot walking slowly back to his plane. Deep in my heart I thought—*it is always the same question: where do we begin to take a stand?* But I turned away.

"No, I'm not a Rastafarian," I said. And true, I am not. But deep inside of me I felt I was being asked to deny some piece of myself, and I felt a solidarity with my Rastafarian brothers and sisters that I had never been conscious of before.

"Is your hair still political?"
Tell me, when it starts to burn.[*]

My immigration card was stamped admit, our bags were put back on the plane, and we continued our journey, twenty minutes overdue. As the plane taxied to the end of the runway, I looked back at the Beef Island Airport.

On this tiny island, I had found another example of Black people being used to testify against other Black people, using our enemies' weapons against each other, judging each other on the color of our skin, the cut of our clothes, the styling of our hair. How long will Black women allow ourselves to be used as instruments of oppression against each other?

On a Black Caribbean island, one Black woman had looked into another Black woman's face and found her unacceptable. Not because of what she did, not because of who she was, not even because of what she believed. But because of how she LOOKED. What does it mean, Black people practicing this kind of self-hatred with one another?

The sun was still shining, but somehow the day seemed less bright.

St. Croix, Virgin Islands
January 10, 1990

---

[*] From "A Question of ESSENCE," in Lorde, *Our Dead Behind Us* (New York: W. W. Norton & Company, 1986).

Difference and Survival

An Address at Hunter College

To those of you who sit here a little bemused and I hope very proud, I speak to you as a poet whose role is always to encourage the intimacy of scrutiny. For I believe that as each one of us learns to bear that intimacy those worse fears which rule our lives and shape our silences begin to lose their power over us.

Last week I asked a number of you if you felt different in any way and each one of you said very quickly and in a similar tone, "Oh no, of course not, I don't consider myself different from anybody else." I think it is not by accident that each of you heard my question as "Are you better than . . ." Yet each of you is sitting here now because in some particular way and time, in some particular place and for whatever reason, you dared to excel, to set yourself apart. And that makes you in this particular place and time, different. It is that difference that I urge you to affirm and to explore lest it someday be used against you and against me. It is within our differences that we are both most powerful and most vulnerable, and some of the most difficult tasks of our lives are the claiming of differences and learning to use those differences for bridges rather than as barriers between us.

In a profit economy which needs groups of outsiders as surplus people, we are programmed to respond to difference in one of three ways: to ignore it by denying the testament of our own senses, "Oh, I never noticed." Or if that is not possible, then we try to neutralize it in one of two ways. If the difference has been defined for us in our introductory courses as good, meaning useful in preserving the status quo, in perpetuating the myth of sameness, then we try to copy it. If the difference is defined as bad, that is revolutionary or threatening, then we try to destroy it. But we have few patterns for relating across differences as equals. And unclaimed, our differences are used against us in the service of separation and confusion, for we view them only in opposition to each other, dominant/subordinate, good/bad, superior/inferior. And of course, so long as the existence of human differences means one must be inferior, the recognition of those differences will be fraught with guilt and danger.

Which differences are positive and which negative are determined for us by a society that has been already established, and so must seek to perpetuate itself, faults as well as virtues.

To excel is considered a positive difference, and so you will be encouraged to think of yourselves as the elite. To be poor, or of Color, or female, or homosexual, or old is considered negative, and so these people are encouraged to think of themselves as surplus. Each of these imposed definitions has a place not in human growth and progress, but in human separation, for they represent the dehumanization of difference.

And certainly there are very real differences between us, of race, sex, age, sexuality, class, vision. But it is not the differences between us that tear us apart, destroying the commonalities we share. Rather, it is our refusal to examine the distortions which arise from their misnaming, and from the illegitimate usage of those differences which can be made when we do not claim them nor define them for ourselves.

Racism. The belief in the inherent superiority of one race over all others and thereby the right to dominance. Ageism. Heterosexism. Elitism. These are some of the distortions created around human differences, all serving the purpose of further separation. It is a lifetime pursuit for each one of us to extract these distortions from our living at the same time as we recognize, reclaim, and define the differences upon which they are imposed, and explore what these differences can teach us about the future we must all share. And we do not have forever. The distortions are endemic in our society, and so we pour energy needed for exposing difference into pretending these differences do not exist, thereby encouraging false and treacherous connections. Or we pretend the differences are insurmountable barriers, which encourages a voluntary isolation. Either way, we do not develop tools for using our differences as springboards for creative change within our lives.

Often, we do not even speak of human difference, which is a comparison of attributes best evaluated by their possible effect and illumination within our lives. Instead, we speak of deviance, which is a judgment upon the relationship between the attribute and some long-fixed and established construct. Somewhere on the edge of all our consciousness there is what I call the mythical norm, which each of us knows within our hearts is "not me." In this society, that norm is usually defined as white, thin, male, young, heterosexual, Christian, and financially secure. It is within this mythical norm that the trappings of power reside. Those of us who stand outside that power, for any reason, often identify one way in which we are different, and we assume that quality to be the primary reason for all oppression. We forget those other distortions around difference, some of which we ourselves may be acting out within our daily lives. For unacknowledged difference robs all of us of each other's energy and creative insight, and creates a false hierarchy.

What does this mean for each one of us? I think it means that I must choose to define my difference as you must choose to define yours, to claim it and to use it as creative before it is defined for you and used to eradicate any future, any change.

You must decide what it means to excel and to persevere beyond competence and why you do it. Or else this ability, this difference defined as good right now because it appears to promise a continuation of safety and sameness, this difference will be used to testify against your creativity, it will be used to cordon off those other differences defined/regarded as bad, improper, or threatening, those differences of race, sex, class, gender, and age, all those ways in which a profit economy defines its excess (different) people. And ultimately, it will be used to truncate your future and mine.

The house of your difference is the longing for your greatest power and your deepest vulnerability. It is an indelible part of your life's arsenal. If you allow your difference, whatever it might be, to be defined for you by imposed externals, then it will be defined to your detriment, always, for that definition must [be] dictated by the need of your society, rather than by a merging between the needs of that society and the human needs of self. But as you acknowledge your difference and examine how you wish to use it and for what—the creative power of difference explored—then you can focus it toward a future which we must each commit ourselves to in some particular way if it is to come to pass at all.

This is not a theoretical discussion. I am talking here about the very fabric of your lives, your dreams, your hopes, your visions, your place upon the earth. All of these will help to determine the shape of your future as they themselves are born from your efforts and pains and triumphs of the past. Cherish them. Learn from them. Our differences are polarities between which can spark possibilities for a future we cannot even now imagine, when we acknowledge that we share a unifying vision, no matter how differently expressed; a vision which supposes a future where we may all flourish, as well as a living earth upon which to support our choices. We must define our differences so that we may someday live beyond them, rather than change them.

So this is a call for each of you to remember herself and himself, to reach for new definitions of that self, and to live intensely. To not settle for the safety of pretended sameness and the false security that sameness seems to offer. To feel the consequences of who you wish to be, lest you bring nothing of lasting worth because you have withheld some piece of the essential, which is you.

And make no mistake; you will be paid well not to feel, not to scrutinize the function of your differences and their meaning, until it will be too late to feel at all. You will be paid in insularity, in poisonous creature comforts, false securities, in the spurious belief that the midnight knock will always be upon somebody else's door. But there is no separate survival.

POETRY

from

The First Cities

(1968)

For Genevieve, Miriam, Clem,
no more words
For Marian, Neal, Ed,
different ones.

A Family Resemblance

My sister has my hair my mouth my eyes
And I presume her trustless.
When she was young, and open to any fever
Wearing gold like a veil of fortune on her face,
She waited through each rain a dream of light.
But the sun came up
Burning our eyes like crystal
Bleaching the sky of promise and
My sister stood
Black, unblessed and unbelieving
Shivering in the first cold show of love.

I saw her gold become an arch
Where nightmare hunted
Down the porches
Of her restless nights.
Now through the echoes of denial
She walks a bleached side of reason
Secret now
My sister never waits,
Nor mourns the gold that wandered from her bed.

My sister has my tongue
And all my flesh unanswered
And I presume her trustless as a stone.

Coal

I

Is the total black, being spoken
From the earth's inside.
There are many kinds of open.
How a diamond comes into a knot of flame
How a sound comes into a word, coloured
By who pays what for speaking.

Some words are open
Like a diamond on glass windows
Singing out within the crash of passing sun
Then there are words like stapled wagers
In a perforated book—buy and sign and tear apart—
And come whatever wills all chances
The stub remains
An ill-pulled tooth with a ragged edge.
Some words live in my throat
Breeding like adders. Others know sun
Seeking like gypsies over my tongue
To explode through my lips
Like young sparrows bursting from shell.
Some words
Bedevil me.

Love is a word another kind of open—
As a diamond comes into a knot of flame
I am black because I come from the earth's inside
Take my word for jewel in your open light.

Now that I Am Forever with Child

How the days went
While you were blooming within me
I remember each upon each—
The swelling changed planes of my body—
And how you first fluttered, then jumped
And I thought it was my heart.

How the days wound down
And the turning of winter
I recall, with you growing heavy
Against the wind. I thought
Now her hands
Are formed, and her hair
Has started to curl
Now her teeth are done
Now she sneezes.
Then the seed opened.
I bore you one morning just before spring—
My head rang like a fiery piston
My legs were towers between which
A new world was passing.

From then
I can only distinguish
One thread within running hours
You . . . flowing through selves
Toward you.

Spring III

Spring is the harshest
Blurring the lines of choice
Until summer flesh
Swallows up all decision.

I remember after the harvest was over
When the thick sheaves were gone
And the bones of the gaunt trees
Uncovered
How the dying of autumn was too easy
To solve our loving.

To a Girl Who Knew What Side Her Bread Was Buttered On

He, through the eyes of the first marauder
Saw her, catch of bright thunder, heaping
Tea and bread for her guardian dead
Crunching the nut-dry words they said
And (thinking the bones were sleeping)
He broke through the muffled afternoon
Calling an end to their ritual's tune
With lightning-like disorder:

Leave the bones, Love! Come away
From these summer breads with the flavour of hay—
Your guards can watch the shards of our catch
Warming *our* bones on some winter's day!

Like an ocean of straws the old bones rose
Fearing the lightning's second death.
There was little time to wonder
At the silence of bright thunder
As, with a smile of pity and stealth
She buttered fresh scones for her guardian bones
And they trampled him into the earth.

Father Son and Holy Ghost

I have not ever seen my fathers grave.
Not that his judgment eyes have been forgotten
Nor his great hands print
On our evening doorknobs
One half turn each night and he would come
Misty from the worlds business
Massive and silent as the whole day's wish, ready
To re-define each of our shapes—
But that now the evening doorknobs
Wait, and do not recognize us as we pass.

Each week a different woman
Regular as his one quick glass each evening—
Pulls up the grass his stillness grows
Calling it weed. Each week
A different woman has my mother's face
And he, who time has
Changeless
Must be amazed, who knew and loved but one.

My father died in silence, loving creation
And well-defined response.
He lived still judgments on familiar things
And died, knowing a January fifteenth that year me.

Lest I go into dust
I have not ever seen my father's grave.

Generation

How the young attempt and are broken
Differs from age to age
We were brown free girls
Love singing beneath their skin
Sun in their hair in their eyes
Sun their fortune
The taste of their young boys' manhood
Swelling like birds in their mouths.

In a careless season of power
We wept out our terrible promise
Now these are the children we try
For temptations that wear our face
And who came back from the latched cities of falsehood
Warning—the road to Nowhere is slippery with our blood
Warning—You need not drink the river to get home
For we purchased bridges with our mothers' bloody gold
We are more than kin who come to share
Not blood, but the bloodiness of failure.

How the young are tempted and betrayed
To slaughter or conformity
Is a turn of the mirror
Time's question only.

If You Come Softly

If you come as softly
As wind within the trees
You may hear what I hear
See what sorrow sees.

If you come as lightly
As threading dew
I will take you gladly
Nor ask more of you.

You may sit beside me
Silent as a breath
Only those who stay dead
Shall remember death.

And if you come I will be silent
Nor speak harsh words to you.
I will not ask you why, now.
Or how, or what you do.

We shall sit here, softly
Beneath two different years
And the rich earth between us
Shall drink our tears.

Suffer the Children

Pity for him who suffers from his waste.
Water that flows from the earth
For lack of roots to hold it
And children who are murdered
Before their lives begin.
Who pays his crops to the sun
When the fields are parched by drought
Will mourn the lost water while waiting another rain.
But who shall dis-inter these girls
To love the women they were to become
Or read the legends written beneath their skin?

Those who loved them remember their child's laughter.
But he whose hate has robbed him of their good
Has yet to weep at night above their graves.

Years roll out and rain shall come again.
But however many girls be brought to sun
Someday
A man will thirst for sleep in his southern night
Seeking his peace where no peace is
And come to mourn these children
Given to the dust.

A Lover's Song

Give me fire and I will sing you morning
Finding you heart
And a birth of fruit
For you, a flame that will stay beauty
Song will take us by the hand
And lead us back to light.

Give me fire and I will sing you evening
Asking you water
And quick breath
No farewell winds like a willow switch
Against my body
But a voice to speak
In a dark room.

Suspension

We entered silence
Before the clock struck

Red wine is caught between the crystal
And your fingers
The air solidifys around your mouth.
Once-wind has sucked the curtains in
Like fright, against the evening wall
Prepared for storm   Before the room
Exhales   Your lips unfold.
Within their sudden opening
I hear the clock
Begin to speak again.

I remember now, with the filled crystal
Shattered, the wind-whipped curtains
Bound, and the cold storm
Finally broken,
How the room felt
When your word was spoken—
Warm
As the center of your palms
And as unfree.

from

Cables to Rage

(1970)

for Elizabeth and Jonno
my presents

Rooming houses are old women

Rooming houses are old women
rocking dark windows into their whens
waiting incomplete circles
rocking
rent office to stoop to
community bathrooms to gas rings
and under-bed boxes of once useful garbage
city issued with a twice-a-month check
the young men next door with their loud midnight parties
and fishy rings left in the bathtub
no longer arouse them
from midnight to mealtime no stops inbetween
light breaking to pass through jumbled up windows
and who was it who married the widow that Buzzie's son messed with?

To Welfare and insult from the slow shuffle
from dayswork to shopping bags heavy with leftovers

Rooming houses
are old women waiting
searching
through their darkening windows
the end or beginning of agony
old women seen through half-ajar doors
hoping
they are not waiting
but being
an entrance to somewhere
unknown and desired
and not new.

Bloodbirth

That which is inside of me screaming
beating about for exit or entry
names the wind, wanting winds' voice
wanting winds' power
it is not my heart
and I am trying to tell this
without art or embellishment
with bits of me flying out in all directions
screams memories old pieces of flesh
struck off like dry bark
from a felled tree, bearing
up or out
holding or bring forth
child or demon
is this birth or exorcism or
the beginning machinery of myself
outlining recalling
my father's business—what I must be
about—my own business
minding.

Shall I split
or be cut down
by a word's complexion or the lack of it
and from what direction
will the opening be made
to show the true face of me
lying exposed and together
my children your children their children
bent on our conjugating business.

Martha

I

Martha this is a catalog of days
passing before you looked again.
Someday you will browse and order them
at will, or in your necessities.

I have taken a house at the Jersey shore
this summer. It is not my house.
Today the lightning bugs came.

On the first day you were dead.
With each breath the skin of your face moved
falling in like crumpled muslin.
We scraped together the smashed image of flesh
preparing a memory. No words.
No words.

On the eighth day
you startled the doctors
speaking from your deathplace
to reassure us that you were trying.

Martha these are replacement days
should you ever need them
given for those you once demanded and never found.
May this trip be rewarding;
no one can fault you again Martha
for answering necessity too well
and the gods who honor hard work
will keep this second coming

free from that lack of choice
which hindered your first journey
to this Tarot house.

They said
no hope no dreaming
accept this case of flesh as evidence
of life without fire
and wrapped you in an electric blanket
kept ten degrees below life.
Fetal hands curled inward on the icy sheets
your bed was so cold
the bruises could not appear.

On the second day I knew you were alive
because the grey flesh of your face
suffered.

I love you and cannot feel you less than Martha
I love you and cannot split this shaved head
from Martha's pushy straightness
asking
In a smash of mixed symbols
How long must I wander here
In this final house of my father?

On the Solstice I was in Providence.
You know this town because you visited friends here.
It rained in Providence on the Solstice—
I remember we passed through here twice
on route Six through Providence to the Cape
where we spent our second summer

trying for peace or equity, even.
It always seemed to be raining
by the time we got to Providence.
The Kirschenbaums live in Providence
and Blossom and Barry
and Frances. And Frances.
Martha I am in love again.
Listen, Frances, I said on the Solstice
our summer has started.
Today we are witches and with enough energy
to move mountains back.
Think of Martha.

Back in my hideous city
I saw you today. Your hair has grown
and your armpits are scented
by some careful attendant.
Your *Testing testing testing*
explosive syllables warning me
Of *The mountain has fallen into dung—*
no Martha remember remember Martha—
Warning
Dead flowers will not come to your bed again.
The sun has started south
our season is over.

Today you opened your eyes, giving
a blue-filmed history to your mangled words.
They help me understand
how you are teaching yourself to learn
again.

I need you need me
le suis Martha I do not speak french kissing
oh Wow, Black and Black . . . Black and . . . beautiful?
Black and becoming
somebody else maybe Erica maybe who sat
in the fourth row behind us in high school
but I never took French with you Martha
and who is this *Madame Erudite*
who is not me?

I find you today in a womb full of patients
blue-robed in various convalescences.
Your eyes are closed you are propped
Into a wheelchair, cornered,
in a parody of resting.
The bright glue of tragedy plasters all eyes
to a television set in the opposite corner
where a man is dying
step by step
in the american ritual going.
Someone has covered you
for this first public appearance
in a hospital gown, a badge of your next step.
Evocative voices flow from the set
and the horror is thick
in this room full of broken and mending receptions.
But no one has told you what it's all about Martha
someone has shot Robert Kennedy
we are drifting closer to what you predicted
and your darkness is indeed speaking
Robert Kennedy is dying Martha
but not you not you not you

he has a bullet in his brain Martha
surgery was never considered for you
since there was no place to start
and no one intended to run you down on a highway
being driven home at 7.30 on a low summer evening
I gave a reading in Harlem that night
and who shall we try for this shaven head now
in the courts of heart Martha
where his murder is televised over and over
with residuals
they have caught the man who shot Robert Kennedy
who was another one of difficult journeys—
he has a bullet in his brain Martha
and much less of a chance than you.

On the first day of July you warned me again
the threads are broken
you darkened into explosive angers and
refused to open your eyes, humming interference
your thoughts are not over Martha
they are you and their task is
to remember Martha
we can help with the other
the mechanics of blood and bone
and you cut through the pain of my words
to warn me again
testing testing whoever passes
must tear out their hearing aids
for the duration
I hear you explaining Neal
my husband whoever must give me a present
he has to give me

himself where I can find him for
where can he look at himself
in the mirror I am making
or over my bed where the window
is locked into battle with a wall?

Now I sit in New Jersey with lightning bugs and
mosquitoes
typing and thinking of you.
Tonight you started seizures
which they say is a temporary relapse
but this lake is far away Martha
and I sit unquiet in New Jersey
and think of you.
I Ching the Book of Changes
says I am impertinent to ask of you obliquely
but I have no direct question
only need.
When I cast an oracle today
it spoke of the Abyssmal again
which of all the Hexagrams
is very difficult but very promising
in it water finds its own level, flowing
out from the lowest point.
And I cast another also that cautioned
the superior man to seek his strength
only in its own season.
Martha what did we learn from our brief season
when the summer grackles rang in my walls?
one and one is too late now
you journey through darkness alone
leafless I sit far from my present house

and the grackles' voices are dying
we shall love each other here if ever at all.

    II

Yes *foolish prejudice lies*
I hear you Martha
that you would never harm my children
but you have forgotten their names
and that you are Elizabeth's godmother.
And you offer me coral rings, watches
even your body
if I will help you sneak home.

No Martha my blood is not muddy my hands
are not dirty to touch
Martha I do not know your night nurse's name
even though she is black
yes I did live in Brighton Beach once
which is almost Rockaway
one bitter winter
but not with your night nurse Martha
and yes I agree this is one hell
of a summer.

No you cannot walk yet Martha
and no the medicines you are given
to quiet your horrors
have not affected your brain
yes it is very hard to think but
it is getting easier and yes Martha
we have loved each other and yes I hope
we still can

no Martha I do not know if we shall ever
sleep in each other's arms again.

III

It is the middle of August and you are alive
to discomfort. You have been moved
into a utility room across the hall
from the critical ward because your screaming
disturbs the other patients
your beside table has been moved also
which means you will be there for a while
a favorite now with the floor nurses
who put up a sign on the utility room door
I'M MARTHA HERE DO NOT FORGET ME
PLEASE KNOCK.
A golden attendant named Sukie
bathes you as you proposition her
she is very pretty and very gentle.
The frontal lobe of the brain governs inhibitions
the damage is after all slight
and they say the screaming will pass.

Your daughter Dorrie promises you
will be as good as new, Mama
who only wants to be *Bad as the old.*

I want some truth good hard truth
a sign of youth
we were all young once we had
a good thing going
now I'm making a plan
for a dead rabbit a rare rabbit.

I am dying goddammit dying am I
Dying?
Death is a word you can say now
pain is mortal
I am dying dying for god's sake won't someone please
get me a doctor PLEASE
your screams beat against our faces as you yell
begging relief from the blank cruelty
of a thousand nurses.
A moment of silence breaks
as you accumulate fresh sorrows
then through your pain-fired face
you slip me a wink

Martha Winked.

Your face straightens into impatience
with the loads of shit you are handed
'You're doing just fine Martha what time is it Martha'
'What did you have for supper tonight Martha'
testing testing whoever passes for Martha
you weary of it.
All the people you must straighten out
pass your bedside in the utility room
bringing you cookies
and hoping
you will be kinder than they were.

Go away Mama and Bubie
for 30 years you made me believe
I was shit you shat out for the asking
but I'm not and you'd better believe it

right now would you kindly
stop rubbing my legs
and GET THE HELL OUT OF HERE.
Next week the Bubie brings Teglach
your old favorite
and will you be kinder Martha
than we were to the shell the cocoon
out of which the you is emerging?

    IV
No one you were can come so close
to death without dying
into another Martha.
I await you
as we all await her
fearing her honesty
fearing
we may neither love nor dismiss
Martha with the dross burned away
fearing
condemnation from the essential.

You cannot get closer to death than this Martha
the nearest you've come to living yourself

Sowing

It is the sink of the afternoon
the children asleep or weary.
I have finished planting the tomatoes
in this brief sun after four days of rain
now there is brown earth under my fingernails
And sun full on my skin
with my head thick as honey
the tips of my fingers are stinging
from the rich earth
but more so from the lack of your body
I have been to this place before
where blood seething commanded
my fingers fresh from the earth
dream of plowing a furrow
whose name should be you.

Making it

My body arcing across your white place
we mingle color and substance
wanting to mantle your cold
I share my face with you
but love becomes a lie
as we suffer through split masks
seeking the other half-self.

We are hung up
in giving
what we wish to be given
ourselves.

On a night of the full moon

I

Out of my flesh that hungers
and my mouth that knows
comes the shape I am seeking
for reason.
The curve of your body
fits my waiting hand
your flesh warm as sunlight
your lips quick as young birds
between your thighs the sweet
sharp taste of limes.

Thus I hold you
frank in my heart's eye
in my skin's knowing
as my fingers conceive your flesh
I feel your stomach
curving against me.

Before the moon wanes again
we shall come together.

II

And I would be the moon
spoken over your beckoning flesh
breaking against reservations
beaching thought
my hands at your high tide
over and under inside you

and the passing of hungers
attended, forgotten.

Darkly risen
the moon speaks
my eyes
judging your roundness
delightful.

from

From a Land Where Other People Live

(1973)

Progress Report

These days
when you do say hello I am never sure
if you are being saucy or experimental or
merely protecting some new position.
Sometimes you gurgle while asleep
and I know tender places still intrigue you.
Now
when you question me on love
shall I recommend a dictionary
or myself?

You are the child of wind and ravens I created
always my daughter
I cannot recognize
the currents where you swim and dart
through my loving
upstream to your final place of birth
but you never tire of hearing
how I crept out of my mother's house
at dawn, with an olive suitcase
crammed with books and fraudulent letters
and an unplayed guitar.

Sometimes I see myself flash through your eyes
in a moment
caught between history and obedience
that moment grows each day
before you comply
as, when did washing dishes

change from privilege to chore?
I watch the hollows deepen above your hips
and wonder if I have taught you Black enough
until I see
all kinds of loving still intrigue you
as you grow more and more
dark
rude and tender
and unfraid.

What you took for granted once
you now refuse to take at all
even I
knock before I enter
the shoals of furious choices
not my own
that flood through your secret reading
nightly, under cover.
I have not yet seen you, but
I hear the pages rustle
from behind closed doors.

Moving Out or
The End of Cooperative Living

I am so glad to be moving
away from this prison for black and white faces
assaulting each other with our joint oppression
competing for who pays the highest price for this privilege
I am so glad I am moving
technicoloured complaints aimed at my head
mash themselves on my door like mosquitoes
sweep like empty ladles through the lobby of my eyes
each time my lips move sideways
the smile shatters
on the in thing that races
dictator through our hallways
on concrete faces on soul compactors
on the rhetoric of incinerators and plastic drapes
for the boiler room
on legends of broken elevators
blowing my morning cool
avoiding me in the corridors
dropping their load on my face down 24 stories
of lives in a spectrumed madhouse
pavillion of gnats and nightmare remembering
once we all saved like beggars
to buy our way into this castle
of fantasy and forever now
I am so glad to be moving.

Last month a tenant was asked to leave
because someone saw him

wandering one morning up and down the tenth floor
with no clothes on
having locked himself out the night before
with the garbage
he could not fit into the incinerator
but it made no difference
the floor captain cut the leads to his cable TV
and he left covered in tangled wires of shame
his apartment was reconsecrated by a fumigator
I am so glad I am moving

Although workmen will descend at $100 an hour
to scrape my breath from the walls
to refinish the air and the floors with their eyes
and charge me with the exact amount
of whatever I have coming back to me
called equity
I am so glad to be moving
from the noise of psychic footsteps
beating a tune that is not my own
louder than any other sound in the neighborhood
except the blasting that goes on all day and all night
from the city's new toilet being built
outside the main entrance
from the spirits who live in the locks
of the other seven doors
bellowing secrets of living hells revealed
but not shared
for everybody's midnights know what the walls hide
our toilets are made of glass
wired for sound

24 stories
full of tears flushing at midnight
our only community room
children set their clocks to listen at the tissue walls
gazing upward from their stools
from one flight to another
catching the neighbors in private struggles
next morning it will all be discussed
at length in the elevators
with no secrets left
I am so glad to be moving
no more coming home at night to dream
of caged puppies
grinding their teeth into cartoonlike faces
that half plead and half snicker
then fold under and vanish
back into snarling strangers
I am so glad I am moving.

But when this grim house goes
slipping into the sewer prepared for it
then this whole city can read
its own obituary
written on the broken record of dreams
of ordinary people
who wanted what they could not get
and so pretended to be someone else
ordinary people having
what they never learned to want
themselves
and so becoming
pretension concretized.

Change of Season

Am I to be cursed forever with becoming
somebody else on the way to myself?

Walking backward I fall
into summers behind me
salt with wanting
lovers or friends a job wider shoes
a cool drink
freshness something to bite into
a place to hide out of the rain
out of the shifting melange of seasons
where the cruel boys I chased
and their skinny dodgeball sisters
flamed and died in becoming
the brown autumn
left in search of who tore the streamers down
at graduation christmas my wedding day
and as winter wore out the babies came
angry effort and reward
in their appointed seasons
my babies tore out of me
like poems
after
I slept and woke to the thought
that promise had come again
this time more sure than the dream of being
sweet sixteen and somebody else
walking five miles through the august city
with a free dog

thinking
now we will be the allamerican family
we had just gotten a telephone
and the next day my sister cut his leash on Broadway
that dog of my childhood bays at the new moon
as I reach into time up to my elbows
extracting the taste and sharp smell
of my first lover's neck
rough as the skin of a brown pear ripening
I was terribly sure I would come forever to april
with my first love who died on a sunday morning
poisoned and wondering
would summer ever come.

As I face an ocean of seasons they start
to separate into distinct and particular faces
listening to the cover beginning to crack open
and whether or not the fruit is worth waiting
thistles and arrows and apples are blooming
the individual beautiful faces are smiling and moving
even the pavement begins to flow into new concretions
the eighth day is coming

I have paid dearly in time for love I hoarded
unseen
summer goes into my words
and comes out reason.

Generation II

A Black girl
going
into the woman
her mother
desired
and prayed for
walks alone
and afraid
of both
their angers.

Love, Maybe

Always
in the middle
of our bloodiest battles
you lay down your arms
like flowering mines

to conqueror me home.

Conclusion

Passing men in the street who are dead
becomes a common occurrence
but loving one of them
is no solution.
I believe in love as I believe in our children
but I was born Black and without illusions
and my vision
which differs from yours
is clear
although sometimes restricted.

I have watched you at midnight
moving through casual sleep
wishing I could afford the non-desperate dreams
that stir you
to wither and fade into partial solutions.
Your nights are wintery long and very young
full of symbols of purity and forgiveness
and a meek jesus that rides through your cities
on a barren ass whose braying
does not include a future tense.
But I wear my nights as I wear my life
and my dying
absolute and unforgiven
nuggets of compromise and decision
fossilized by fierce midsummer sun
and when I dream
I move through a Black land
where the future

glows eternal and green
but where the symbols for now
are bloody and unrelenting
rooms
where confused children
with wooden stumps for fingers
play at war
who cannot pick up their marbles
and run away home
whenever nightmare threatens.

Movement Song

I have studied the tight curls on the back of your neck
moving away from me
beyond anger or failure
your face in the evening schools of longing
through mornings of wish and ripen
we were always saying goodbye
in the blood in the bone over coffee
before dashing for elevators going
in opposite directions
without goodbyes.

Do not remember me as a bridge nor a roof
as the maker of legends
nor as a trap
door to that world
where black and white clericals
hang on the edge of beauty in five oclock elevators
twitching their shoulders to avoid other flesh
and now
there is someone to speak for them
moving away from me into tomorrows
morning of wish and ripen
your goodbye is a promise of lightning
in the last angels hand
unwelcome and warning
the sands have run out against us
we were rewarded by journeys
away from each other
into desire

into mornings alone
where excuse and endurance mingle
conceiving decision.
Do not remember me
as disaster
nor as the keeper of secrets
I am a fellow rider in the cattle cars
watching
you move slowly out of my bed
saying we cannot waste time
only ourselves.

Who Said
It Was Simple

There are so many roots to the tree of anger
that sometimes the branches shatter
before they bear.

Sitting in Nedicks
the women rally before they march
discussing the problematic girls
they hire to make them free.
An almost white counterman passes
a waiting brother to serve them first
and the ladies neither notice nor reject
the slighter pleasures of their slavery.
But I who am bound by my mirror
as well as my bed
see causes in colour
as well as sex

and sit here wondering
which me will survive
all these liberations.

from

New York
Head Shop and
Museum

(1974)

TO THE CHOCOLATE PEOPLE OF AMERICA

Chocolate people don't melt in water
they melt in your eyes.
                    Jonathan Rollins—1971

New York City 1970

I

How do you spell change like frayed slogan underwear
with the emptied can of yesterdays' meanings
with yesterdays' names?
And what does the we-bird see with
who has lost its I's?

There is nothing beautiful left in the streets of this city.
I have come to believe in death and renewal by fire.
Past questioning the necessities of blood
or why it must be mine or my children's time
that will see the grim city quake to be reborn perhaps
blackened again but this time with a sense of purpose;
tired of the past tense forever, of assertion and repetition
of the ego-trips through an incomplete self
where two years ago proud rang for promise but now
it is time for fruit and all the agonies are barren—
only the children are growing:

For how else can the self become whole
save by making self into its own new religion?
I am bound like an old lover—a true believer—
to this city's death by accretion and slow ritual,
and I submit to its penance for a trial
as new steel is tried
I submit my children also to its death throes and agony
and they are not even the city's past lovers. But I submit them
to the harshness and growing cold to the brutalizations
which if survived

will teach them strength or an understanding of how strength
    is gotten
and will not be forgotten: It will be their city then:
I submit them
loving them above all others save myself
to the fire to the rage to the ritual scarifications
to be tried as new steel is tried;
and in its wasting the city shall try them
as the blood-splash of a royal victim
tries the hand of the destroyer.

II

I hide behind tenements and subways in fluorescent alleys
watching as flames walk the streets of an empire's altar
raging through the veins of the sacrificial stenchpot
smeared upon the east shore of a continent's insanity
conceived in the psychic twilight of murderers and pilgrims
rank with money and nightmare and too many useless people
who will not move over nor die, who cannot bend
even before the winds of their own preservation
even under the weight of their own hates
Who cannot amend nor conceive nor even learn to share
their own visions
who bomb my children into mortar in churches
and work plastic offal and metal and the flesh of their enemies
into subway rush-hour temples where obscene priests
finger and worship each other in secret
and think they are praying when they squat
to shit money-pebbles shaped like their parents' brains—
who exist to go into dust to exist again
grosser and more swollen and without ever relinquishing
space or breath or energy from their private hoard.

I do not need to make war nor peace
with these prancing and murderous deacons
who refuse to recognize their role in this covenant we live upon
and so have come to fear and despise even their own children;
but I condemn myself, and my loves
past and present
and the blessed enthusiasms of all my children
to this city
without reason or future
without hope
to be tried as the new steel is tried
before trusted to slaughter.

I walk down the withering limbs of my last discarded house
and there is nothing worth salvage left in this city
but the faint reedy voices like echoes
of once beautiful children.

The American Cancer Society Or There Is More Than One Way To Skin A Coon

Of all the ways in which this country
Prints its death upon me
Selling me cigarettes is one of the most certain.
Yet every day I watch my son digging
ConEdison GeneralMotors GarbageDisposal
Out of his nose as he watches a 3 second spot
On How To Stop Smoking
And it makes me sick to my stomach.
For it is not by cigarettes
That you intend to destroy my children.

Not even by the cold white light of moon-walks
While half the boys I knew
Are doomed to quicker trips by a different capsule;
No, the american cancer destroys
By seductive and reluctant admission
For instance
Black women no longer give birth through their ears
And therefore must have A Monthly Need For Iron:
For instance
Our Pearly teeth are *not* racially insured
And therefore must be Gleemed For Fewer Cavities:
For instance
Even though all astronauts are white
Perhaps Black People *can* develop
Some of those human attributes

Requiring
Dried dog food frozen coffee instant oatmeal
Depilatories deodorants detergents
And other assorted plastic.

And this is the surest sign I know
That the american cancer society is dying—
It has started to dump its symbols onto Black People
Convincing proof that those symbols are now useless
And far more lethal than emphysema.

A Sewerplant Grows In Harlem
Or
I'm A Stranger Here Myself
When Does The Next Swan Leave

How is the word made flesh made steel made shit
by ramming it into No Exit like a homemade bomb
until it explodes
smearing itself
made real
against our already filthy windows
or by flushing it out in a verbal fountain?
Meanwhile the editorial They—
who are no less powerful—
prepare to smother the actual Us
with a processed flow of all our shit
non-verbal.

Have you ever risen in the night
bursting with knowledge and the world
dissolves toward any listening ear
into which you can pour
whatever it was you knew
before waking
Only to find all ears asleep
or drugged perhaps by a dream of words
because as you scream into them over and over
nothing stirs
and the mind you have reached is not a working mind
please hang up and die again? The mind

you have reached is not a working mind
Please hang up
And die again.

Talking to some people is like talking to a toilet.

One Year To Life On
The Grand Central Shuttle

If we hate the rush hour subways
who ride them every day
why hasn't there been a New York City Subway Riot
some bloody rush-hour revolution
where a snarl
goes on from push to a shove
that does not stop
at the platform's edge
the whining of automated trains
will drown out the screams
of our bloody and releasing testament
to a last chance or hope of change.

But hope is counter-revolutionary.
Pressure cooks
but we have not exploded
flowing in and out instead each day
like a half-digested mass
for a final stake impales our dreams
and watering down each trip's fury
is the someday foolish hope
that at the next stop
some door will open for us
to fresh air and light and home.

When we realize how
much of us is spent

in rush hour subways
underground
no real exit
it will matter less
what token we pay
for change.

The Workers Rose On May Day
Or
Postscript To Karl Marx

Down Wall Street
the students marched for peace
Above, construction workers looking on remembered
how it was for them in the old days
before their closed shop white security
and daddy pays the bills
so they climbed down the girders
and taught their sons a lesson
called Marx is a victim of the generation gap
called I grew up the hard way so will you
called
the limits of a sentimental vision.

When the passion play was over
and the dust had cleared on Wall Street
500 Union workers together with police
had mopped up Foley Square
with 2000 of their striking sons
who broke and ran
before their fathers chains.

Look here Karl Marx
the apocalyptic vision of amerika!
Workers rise and win
and have not lost their chains
but swing them

side by side with the billyclubs in blue
securing Wall Street
against the striking students.

Cables to Rage
or
I've Been Talking on This Street
Corner a Hell of a Long Time

This is how I came to be loved
by loving myself loveless.

One day I slipped in the snowy gutter of Brighton Beach
and the booted feet passing
me by on the curb squished my laundry ticket
into the slush and I thought oh fuck it now
I'll never get my clean sheet and I cried bitter tears
into the snow under my cheek in that gutter in Brighton Beach
Brooklyn where I was living because it was cheap

In a furnished room with cooking privileges
and there was an old thrown-away mama who lived down the hall
a yente who sat all day long in our common kitchen
weeping because her children made her live with a schwartze
and while she wept she drank up all my Cream Soda
every day before I came home.
Then she sat and watched me watching my chicken feet stewing
on the Fridays when I got paid
and she taught me to boil old corn in the husk
to make it taste green and fresh.
There were not many pleasures in that winter
and I loved Cream Soda
there were not many people in that winter
and I came to hate that old woman.

The winter I got fat on stale corn on the cob
and chicken foot stew and the day before Christmas
having no presents to wrap
I poured two ounces of Nux Vomica into a bottle of Cream Soda
and listened to the old lady puke all night long.
When spring came I crossed the river again
moving up in the world six and half stories
and one day on the corner of eighth street across from Wanamakers
which had burned down while I was away in Brooklyn—
where I caught the bus for work every day
a bus driver slowed down at the bus stop one morning—
I was late it was raining and my jacket was soaked—
and then speeded past without stopping when he saw my face.

I have been given other doses of truth—
that particular form of annihilation—
shot through by the cold eye of the way things are baby
and left for dead on a hundred streets of this city
but oh that captain marvel glance
brushing up against my skull like a steel bar
in passing
and my heart withered sheets in the gutter
passing passing
booted feet and bus drivers
and old yentes in Brighton Beach kitchens
SHIT! said the king and the whole court strained
passing
me out as an ill-tempered wind
lashing around the corner
of 125th Street and Lenox.

Keyfood

In the Keyfood Market on Broadway
a woman waits
by the window
daily and patient
the comings and goings of buyers
neatly labeled old
like yesterday's bread
her restless experienced eyes
weigh fears like grapefruit
testing for ripeness.

Once in the market
she was more
comfortable than wealthy
more black than white
more proper than friendly
more rushed than alone
all her powers defined her
like a carefully kneaded loaf
rising and restrained
working and making loving
behind secret eyes.

Once she was all
the sums of her knowing
counting on her to sustain them
once she was more
somebody else's mother than mine

now she weighs faces
as once she weighed grapefruit.

Waiting
she does not count her change
Her lonely eyes measure
all who enter the market
are they new
are they old
enough
can they buy each other?

To The Girl Who Lives In A Tree

A letter in my mailbox says you've made it
to Honduras and I wonder what is the colour
of the wood you are chopping now.

When you left this city I wept for a year
down 14th Street across the Taconic Parkway
through the shingled birdcotes along Riverside Drive
and I was glad because in your going
you left me a new country
where Riverside Drive became an embattlement
that even dynamite could not blast free
where making both love and war became less inconsistent
and as my tears watered morning I became
my own place to fathom
While part of me follows you still thru the woods of Oregon
splitting dead wood with a rusty axe
acting out the nightmares of your mothers
creamy skin soot-covered from communal fires
where you provide and labour to discipline your dreams
whose symbols are immortalized in lies of history
told like fairy tales called power
behind the throne called noble frontier drudge and
we both know you are not white
with rage or fury but only from bleeding
too much while trudging behind a wagon and confidentially
did you really conquer Donner Pass with only a handcart?

My mothers nightmares are not yours but just as binding.
If in your sleep you tasted a child's blood on your teeth

while your chained black hand could not rise
to wipe away his death upon your lips
perhaps you would consider then
why I choose this brick and shitty stone
over the good earth's challenge of green.
Your mothers nightmares are not mine but just as binding.
We share more than a trap between our legs
where long game howl back and forth across country
finding less than what they bargained for
but more than they ever feared
so dreams or not, I think you will be back soon from Honduras
where the woods are even thicker than in Oregon.
You will see it finally as a choice too
between loving women or loving trees
and if only from the standpoint of free movement
women win
hands down.

Love Poem

Speak earth and bless me with what is richest
make sky flow honey out of my hips
rigid as mountains
spread over a valley
carved out by the mouth of rain.

And I knew when I entered her I was
high wind in her forests hollow
fingers whispering sound
honey flowed
from the split cup
impaled on a lance of tongues
on the tips of her breasts on her navel
and my breath
howling into her entrances
through lungs of pain.

Greedy as herring-gulls
or a child
I swing out over the earth
over and over
again.

Separation

The stars dwindle
and will not reward me
even in triumph.

It is possible
to shoot a man
in self defense
and still notice
how his red blood
decorates the snow.

Song For A Thin Sister

Either heard or taught
as girls
we thought
that skinny was funny
or a little bit
silly
and feeling a pull
toward the large and the colorful
I would joke you
when
you grew too thin.

But your new kind of hunger
makes me chilly
like danger
for I see you forever retreating
shrinking
into a stranger
in flight—
and
growing up
black and fat
I was so sure
that skinny was funny
or silly
but always
white.

Revolution Is One Form
Of Social Change

When the man is busy
making niggers
it doesn't matter
much
what shade
you are.

If he runs out of one
particular color
he can always switch
to size
and when he's finished
off the big ones
he'll just change
to sex
which is
after all
where it all began.

The Brown Menace
Or
Poem To The Survival
of Roaches

Call me
your deepest urge
toward survival
call me
and my brothers and sisters
in the sharp smell of your refusal
call me
roach and presumptious
nightmare on your white pillow
your itch to destroy
the indestructible
part of yourself.

Call me
your own determination
in the most detestable shape
you can become
friend of your image
within me
I am you
in your most deeply cherished nightmare
scuttling through the painted cracks
you create to admit me
into your kitchens
into your fearful midnights

into your values at noon
in your most secret places
with hate
you learn to honor me
by imitation
as I alter—
through your greedy preoccupations
through your kitchen wars
and your poisonous refusal—
to survive.

To survive.
Survive.

Sacrifice

The only hungers left
are the hungers allowed us.

By the light of our sacred street lamps
by whatever maps we are sworn to follow
pleasure will betray us
unless we do what we must do
without
wanting to do it
feel the enemy stone give way in retreat
without pleasure or satisfaction
we look the other way
as our dreams come true
as our bloody hands move over history
writing
we have come
we have done
what we came to do.

Pulling down statues of rock from their high places
we must level the expectation
upon which they stand
waiting for us
to fulfill their image
waiting
for our feet to replace them.

Unless we refuse to sleep
even one night in houses of marble

the sight of our children's false pleasure
will undo us
for our children have grown
in the shadow of what was
the shape of marble
between their eyes and the sun
but we do not wish to stand
like great marble statues
between our children's eyes
and their sun.

Learning all
we can use
only what is vital
The only sacrifice of worth
is the sacrifice of desire.

from

Between
Our Selves

(1976)

for Frances

*for the embattled
there is no place
that cannot be
home.
nor is.*

Power

The difference between poetry and rhetoric
is being ready to kill
yourself
instead of your children.

I am trapped on a desert of raw gunshot wounds
and a dead child dragging his shattered black
face off the edge of my sleep
blood from his punctured cheeks and shoulders
is the only liquid for miles
and my stomach
churns at the imagined taste while
my mouth splits into dry lips
without loyalty or reason
thirsting for the wetness of his blood
as it sinks into the whiteness
of the desert where I am lost
without imagery or magic
trying to make power out of hatred and destruction
trying to heal my dying son with kisses
only the sun will bleach his bones quicker.

A policeman who shot down a ten year old in Queens
stood over the boy with his cop shoes in childish blood
and a voice said "Die you little motherfucker" and
there are tapes to prove it. At his trial
this policeman said in his own defense
"I didn't notice the size nor nothing else

only the color". And
there are tapes to prove that, too.

Today that 37 year old white man
with 13 years of police forcing
was set free
by eleven white men who said they were satisfied
justice had been done
and one Black Woman who said
"They convinced me" meaning
they had dragged her 4'10" Black Woman's frame
over the hot coals
of four centuries of white male approval
until she let go
the first real power she ever had
and lined her own womb with cement
to make a graveyard for our children.

I have not been able to touch the destruction
within me.
But unless I learn to use
the difference between poetry and rhetoric
my power too will run corrupt as poisonous mold
or lie limp and useless as an unconnected wire
and one day I will take my teenaged plug
and connect it to the nearest socket
raping an 85 year old white woman
who is somebody's mother
and as I beat her senseless and set a torch to her bed
a greek chorus will be singing in 3/4 time
"Poor thing. She never hurt a soul. What beasts they are."

Solstice

We forgot to water the plantain shoots
when our houses were full of borrowed meat
and our stomachs with the gift of strangers
who laugh now as they pass us
because our land is barren
the farms are choked
with stunted rows of straw
and with our nightmares of juicy brown yams
that cannot fill us.
The roofs of our houses rot from last winter's water
but our drinking pots are broken
we have used them to mourn the death of old lovers
the next rain will wash our footprints away
and our children have married beneath them.

Our skins are empty.
They have been vacated by the spirits
who are angered by our reluctance
to feed them
in baskets of straw made from sleep grass
and the droppings of civets
they have been hidden away by our mothers
who are waiting for us at the river.

My skin is tightening
soon I shall shed it
like a monitor lizard
like remembered comfort

at the new moons rising
I will eat the last signs of my weakness
remove the scars of old childhood wars
and dare to enter the forest whistling
like a snake that had fed the chameleon
for changes
I shall be forever.

May I never remember reasons
for my spirit's safety
may I never forget
the warning of my woman's flesh
weeping at the new moon
may I never lose
that terror
which keeps me brave
may I owe nothing
that I cannot repay.

Scar

This is a simple poem.
For the mothers sisters daughters
girls I have never been
for the women who clean the Staten Island Ferry
for the sleek witches who burn
me at midnight
in effigy
because I eat at their tables
and sleep with their ghosts.

These stones in my heart are you
of my own flesh
whittling me with your sharp false eyes
searching for prisms
falling out of your head
laughing me out of your skin
because you do not value your own
self
nor me.

This is a simple poem
I will have no mother no sister no daughter
when I am through
and only the bones are left
see how the bones are showing
the shape of us at war
clawing our own flesh out
to feed the backside of our masklike faces
that we have given the names of men.

Donald DeFreeze I never knew you so well
as in the eyes of my own mirror
did you hope
for blessing or pardon
lying
in bed after bed
or was your eye sharp and merciless enough
to endure
beyond the deaths of wanting?

With your voice in my ears
with my voice in your ears
try to deny me
I will hunt you down
through the night veins of my own addiction
through all my unsatisfied childhoods
as this poem unfolds
like the leaves of a poppy
I have no sister no mother no children
left
only a tideless ocean of moonlit women
in all shades of loving
learning a dance of open and closing
learning a dance of electrical tenderness
no father no mother would teach them.

Come Sambo dance with me
pay the piper dangling dancing
his knee high darling
over your wanting
under your bloody
white faces come Bimbo come Ding Dong

watch the city falling down down
down lie down bitch slow down nigger
so you want a cozy womb to hide you
to pucker up and suck you back
safely
well I tell you what I'm gonna do
next time you head for the hatchet
really need some nook to hole up in
look me up
I'm the ticket taker on a queen
of rollercoasters
I can get you off
cheap.

This is a simple poem
sharing my head with the dream
of a big black woman with jewels
in her eyes
she dances
her head in a golden helmet
arrogant
plumed
her name is Colossa
her thighs are like stanchions
or flayed hickory trees
embraced in armour
she dances
in slow earth shaking motions
that suddenly alter
and lighten
as she whirls laughing
tooled metal over her hips

comes to an end
and at the shiny edge
an astonishment
of soft black curly hair.

Between Ourselves

Once when I walked into a room
my eyes would seek out the one or two black faces
for contact or reassurance or a sign
I was not alone
now walking into rooms full of black faces
that would destroy me for any difference
where shall my eyes look?
Once it was easy to know
who were my people.

If we were stripped of all pretense
to our strength
and our flesh was cut away
the sun would bleach all our bones
as white
as the face of my black mother
was bleached white by gold
or Orishala
and how
does that measure me?

I do not believe
our wants have made all our lies
holy.

Under the sun on the shores of Elmina
a black man sold the woman who carried
my grandmother in her belly
he was paid with bright yellow coins

that shone in the evening sun
and in the faces of her sons and daughters.
When I see that brother behind my eyes
his irises are bloodless and without colour
his tongue clicks like yellow coins
tossed up on this shore
where we share the same corner
of an alien and corrupted heaven
and whenever I try to eat
the words
of easy blackness as salvation
I taste the colour
of my grandmother's first betrayal.

I do not believe
our wants
have made all our lies
holy.

But I do not whistle this man's name
at the shrine of Shopona
I cannot bring down the rosy juices of death upon him
nor forget Orishala
is called the god of whiteness
who works in the dark wombs of night
forming the shapes we all wear
so that even cripples and dwarfs and albinos
are sacred worshippers
when the boiled corn is offered.

Humility lies
in the face of history

and I have forgiven myself
for him
for the white meat
we all consumed in secret
before we were born
we shared the same meal.
When you impale me
upon your lances of narrow blackness
before you hear my heart speak
mourn your own borrowed blood
your own borrowed visions
singing through a foreign tongue.
Do not mistake my flesh
for the enemy
do not write my name in the dust
before the shrine of the god of smallpox
for we are all children of Eshu
god of chance and the unpredictable
and we each wear many changes
inside of our skin.

Armed with scars
healed
in many different colours
I look into my own faces
as Eshu's daughter
crying
if we do not stop killing
the other
in ourselves
the self that we hate
in others

soon we shall all lie
in the same direction
and Eshidale's priests will be very busy
they who alone can bury
all those who seek their own death
by jumping up from the ground
and landing upon their heads.

from

The Black
Unicorn

(1978)

For
Linda Gertrude Belmar Lorde

and
Frederick Byron Lorde

The Face Has Many Seasons

A Woman Speaks

Moon marked and touched by sun
my magic is unwritten
but when the sea turns back
it will leave my shape behind.
I seek no favor
untouched by blood
unrelenting as the curse of love
permanent as my errors
or my pride
I do not mix
love with pity
nor hate with scorn
and if you would know me
look into the entrails of Uranus
where the restless oceans pound.

I do not dwell
within my birth nor my divinities
who am ageless and half-grown
and still seeking
my sisters
witches in Dahomey
wear me inside their coiled cloths
as our mother did
mourning.

I have been woman
for a long time

beware my smile
I am treacherous with old magic
and the noon's new fury
with all your wide futures
promised
I am
woman
and not white.

Coniagui Women

The Coniagui women
wear their flesh like war
bear children who have eight days
to choose their mothers
it is up to the children
who must decide to stay.

Boys burst from the raised loins
twisting and shouting
from the bush secret
they run
beating the other women
avoiding the sweet flesh
hidden
near their mother's fire
but they must take her blood as a token
the wild trees have warned them
beat her and you will be free
on the third day
they creep up to her cooking pot
bubbling over the evening's fire
and she feeds them
yam soup
and silence.

"Let us sleep in your bed" they whisper
"Let us sleep in your bed" they whisper
"Let us sleep in your bed"

but she has mothered before them.
She closes her door.

They become men.

Chain

News item: Two girls, fifteen and sixteen, were sent to foster
homes, because they had borne children by their natural father.
Later, they petitioned the New York courts to be returned to their
parents, who, the girls said, loved them. And the courts did so.

I

Faces surround me that have no smell or color no time
only strange laughing testaments
vomiting promise like love
but look at the skeleton children
advancing against us
beneath their faces there is no sunlight
no darkness
no heart remains
no legends
to bring them back as women
into their bodies at dawn.

Look at the skeleton children
advancing against us
we will find womanhood
in their eyes
as they cry
which of you bore me
will love me
will claim my blindness as yours
and which of you marches to battle
from between my legs?

II

On the porch outside my door
girls are lying
like felled maples in the path of my feet
I cannot step past them nor over them
their slim bodies roll like smooth tree trunks
repeating themselves over and over
until my porch is covered with the bodies
of young girls.
Some have a child in their arms.
To what death shall I look for comfort?
Which mirror to break or mourn?

Two girls repeat themselves in my doorway
their eyes are not stone.
Their flesh is not wood nor steel
but I can not touch them.
Shall I warn them of night
or offer them bread
or a song?
They are sisters. Their father has known
them over and over. The twins they carry
are his. Whose death shall we mourn
in the forest
unburied?
Winter has come and the children are dying.

One begs me to hold her between my breasts
Oh write me a poem mother
here, over my flesh
get your words upon me
as he got this child upon me

our father lover
thief in the night
do not be so angry with us. We told him
your bed was wider
but he said if we did it then
we would be his
good children if we did it
then he would love us
oh make us a poem mother
that will tell us his name
in your language
is he father or lover
we will leave your word
for our children
engraved on a whip or a golden scissors
to tell them the lies
of their birth.
Another says mother
I am holding your place.
Do you know me better than I knew him
or myself?
Am I his daughter or girlfriend
am I your child or your rival
you wish to be gone from his bed?
Here is your granddaughter mother
give us your blessing before I sleep
what other secrets
do you have to tell me
how do I learn to love her
as you have loved me?

Sequelae

Because a burning sword notches both of my doorposts
because I am standing between
my burned hands in the ashprint of two different houses
midnight finds weave a filigree of disorder
I figure in the dreams of people
who do not even know me
the night is a blister of stars
pierced by nightmares of a telephone ringing
my hand is the receiver
threatening as an uncaged motor
seductive as the pain of voiceless mornings
voiceless kitchens I remember
cornflakes shrieking like banshees in my throat
while I battle the shapes of you
wearing old ghosts of me
hating you for being
black and not woman
hating you for being white
and not me
in this carnival of memories
I name you both the laying down of power
the separation I cannot yet make
after all these years of blood
my eyes are glued
like fury to the keyholes
of yesterday
rooms
where I wander
solitary as a hunting cheetah

at play with legends call disaster
due all women who refuse to wait
in vain;

In a new room
I enter old places bearing your shape
trapped behind the sharp smell of your anger
in my voice
behind tempting invitations
to believe
your face
tipped like a pudding under glass
and I hear the high pitch of your voice
crawling out from my hearts
deepest culverts
compromise is a coffin nail
rusty as seaweed
tiding through an august house
where nobody lives
beyond choice
my pathways are strewn with old discontents
outgrown defenses still sturdy as firebrick
unlovely and dangerous as measles
they wither into uselessness
but do not decay.

Because I do not wish
to remember
but love to caress the deepest bone
of me
begging shes that wax and wane like moonfire
to absolve me at any price

I battle old ghosts of you
wearing the shapes of me
surrounded by black
and white faces
saying no over and over
becoming my mother draped in my fathers
bastard ambition
growing dark secrets
out from between her thighs
and night comes into me like a fever
my hands grip a flaming sword that screams
while an arrogant woman masquerading as a fish
plunges it deeper and deeper
into the heart we both share
like beggars
on this moment of time
where the space ships land
I have died too many deaths
that were not mine.

A Litany for Survival

For those of us who live at the shoreline
standing upon the constant edges of decision
crucial and alone
for those of us who cannot indulge
the passing dreams of choice
who love in doorways coming and going
in the hours between dawns
looking inward and outward
at once before and after
seeking a now that can breed
futures
like bread in our children's mouths
so their dreams will not reflect
the death of ours;

For those of us
who were imprinted with fear
like a faint line in the center of our foreheads
learning to be afraid with our mother's milk
for by this weapon
this illusion of some safety to be found
the heavy-footed hoped to silence us
For all of us
this instant and this triumph
We were never meant to survive.

And when the sun rises we are afraid
it might not remain
when the sun sets we are afraid

it might not rise in the morning
when our stomachs are full we are afraid
of indigestion
when our stomachs are empty we are afraid
we may never eat again
when we are loved we are afraid
love will vanish
when we are alone we are afraid
love will never return
and when we speak we are afraid
our words will not be heard
nor welcomed
but when we are silent
we are still afraid.

So it is better to speak
remembering
we were never meant to survive.

Portrait

Strong women
know the taste
of their own hatred
I must always be
building nests
in a windy place
I want the safety of oblique numbers
that do not include me
a beautiful woman
with ugly moments
secret and patient
as the amused and ponderous elephants
catering to Hannibal's ambition
as they swayed on their own way
home.

Therapy

Trying to see you
my eyes grow
confused
it is not your face
they are seeking
fingering through your spaces
like a hungry child
even now
I do not want
to make a poem
I want to make you
more and less
a part
from my self.

Recreation

Coming together
it is easier to work
after our bodies
meet
paper and pen
neither care nor profit
whether we write or not
but as your body moves
under my hands
charged and waiting
we cut the leash
you create me against your thighs
hilly with images
moving through our word countries
my body
writes into your flesh
the poem
you make of me.

Touching you I catch midnight
as moon fires set in my throat
I love you flesh into blossom
I made you
and take you made
into me.

Artisan

In workshops without light
we have made birds
that do not sing
kites that shine
but cannot fly
with the speed
by which light falls
in the throat
of delicate working fire
I thought I had discovered
a survival kit
buried
in the moon's heart
flat and resilient as turtles
a case of tortoise shell
hung
in the mouth of darkness
precise unlikely markings
carved into the carapace
sweet meat beneath.

I did not recognize
the shape
of my own name.

Our bed spread
is a midnight flower
coming

all the way down
to the floor
there
your craft shows.

Contact Lenses

Lacking what they want to see
makes my eyes hungry
and eyes can feel
only pain.

Once I lived behind thick walls
of glass
and my eyes belonged
to a different ethic
timidly rubbing the edges
of whatever turned them on.
Seeing usually
was a matter of what was
in front of my eyes
matching what was
behind my brain.
Now my eyes have become
a part of me exposed
quick risky and open
to all the same dangers.

I see much
better now
and my eyes hurt.

But What Can You Teach My Daughter

What do you mean
no no no no
you don't have the right
to know
how often
have we built each other
as shelters
against the cold
and even my daughter knows
what you know
can hurt you
she says her nos
and it hurts
she says
when she talks of liberation
she means freedom
from that pain
she knows
what you know
can hurt
but what you do
not know
can kill.

From Inside an Empty Purse

Money cannot buy you
what you want
standing flatfooted
and lying
like a grounded chestnut
unlovable and suspect
I am trying to reach
you
on whatever levels
you flow from
treacherous growing
water
in a blind tongueless pond.

I am the thread of your woman's cloth
the sexy prison that protects you
deep and unspoken
flesh around your freedom
I am your enemy's face.

The money doesn't matter
so much
as the lie
telling
you don't know
why
in a dream
I am trying to reach
you before
you fall in
to me.

A Small Slaughter

Day breaks without thanks or caution
past a night without satisfaction or pain.
My words are blind children I have armed
against the casual insolence of morning
without you
I am scarred and marketed
like a streetcorner in Harlem
a woman
whose face in the tiles
your feet have not yet regarded
I am the stream
past which you will never step
the woman you can not deal with
I am the mouth
of your scorn.

Sister Outsider

We were born in a poor time
never touching
each other's hunger
never
sharing our crusts
in fear
the bread became enemy.

Now we raise our children
to respect themselves
as well as each other.

Now you have made loneliness
holy and useful
and no longer needed
now
your light shines very brightly
but I want you
to know
your darkness also
rich
and beyond fear.

"Never Take Fire
from a Woman"

My sister and I
have been raised to hate
genteelly
each other's silences
sear up our tongues
like flame
we greet each other
with respect
meaning
from a watchful distance
while we dream of lying
in the tender of passion
to drink from a woman
who smells like love.

Between Ourselves

Once when I walked into a room
my eyes would seek out the one or two black faces
for contact or reassurance or a sign
I was not alone
now walking into rooms full of black faces
that would destroy me for any difference
where shall my eyes look?
Once it was easy to know
who were my people.

If we were stripped to our strength
of all pretense
and our flesh was cut away
the sun would bleach all our bones as white
as the face of my black mother
was bleached white by gold
or Orishala
and how
does that measure me?

I do not believe
our wants have made all our lies
holy.

Under the sun on the shores of Elmina
a black man sold the woman who carried
my grandmother in her belly
he was paid with bright yellow coin
that shone in the evening sun
and in the faces of her sons and daughters.

When I see that brother behind my eyes
his irises are bloodless and without color
his tongue clicks like yellow coins
tossed up on this shore
where we share the same corner
of an alien and corrupted heaven
and whenever I try to eat
the words
of easy blackness as salvation
I taste the color
of my grandmother's first betrayal.

I do not believe
our wants
have made all our lies
holy.

But I do not whistle his name at the shrine of Shopona
I do not bring down the rosy juices of death upon him
nor forget Orishala
is called the god of whiteness
who works in the dark wombs of night
forming the shapes we all wear
so that even cripples and dwarfs and albinos
are scared worshipers
when the boiled corn is offered.

Humility lies
in the face of history
I have forgiven myself
for him
for the white meat
we all consumed in secret

before we were born
we shared the same meal.
When you impale me
upon your lances of narrow blackness
before you hear my heart speak
mourn your own borrowed blood
your own borrowed visions
Do not mistake my flesh for the enemy
do not write my name in the dust
before the shrine of the god of smallpox
for we are all children of Eshu
god of chance and the unpredictable
and we each wear many changes
inside of our skin.

Armed with scars
healed
in many different colors
I look in my own faces
as Eshu's daughter crying
if we do not stop killing
the other
in ourselves
the self that we hate
in others
soon we shall all lie
in the same direction
and Eshidale's priests will be very busy
they who alone can bury
all those who seek their own death
by jumping up from the ground
and landing upon their heads.

from

Chosen Poems:
Old and New

(1982)

To Frances Louise Clayton

our footsteps hold this place together
our decisions make the possible whole.

The Evening News

First rule of the road: attend quiet victims first.

I am kneading my bread Winnie Mandela
while children who sing in the streets of Soweto
are jailed for inciting to riot
the moon in Soweto is mad
is bleeding my sister into the earth
is mixing her seed with the vultures'
greeks reap her like olives out of the trees
she is skimmed like salt
from the skin of a hungry desert
while the Ganvie fisherwomen with milk-large breasts
hide a fish with the face of a small girl
in the prow of their boats.

Winnie Mandela I am feeling your face
with pain of my crippled fingers
our children are escaping their births
in the streets of Soweto and Brooklyn
(what does it mean
our wars
being fought by our children?)

Winnie Mandela our names are like olives, salt, sand
the opal, amber, obsidian that hide their shape well.
We have never touched shaven foreheads together
yet how many of our sisters' and daughters' bones
whiten in secret

whose names we have not yet spoken
whose names we have never spoken
I have never heard their names spoken.

*Second rule of the road: any wound will stop bleeding if
you press down hard enough.*

Afterimages

I

However the image enters
its force remains within
my eyes
rockstrewn caves where dragonfish evolve
wild for life, relentless and acquisitive
learning to survive
where there is no food
my eyes are always hungry
and remembering
however the image enters
its force remains.
A white woman stands bereft and empty
a black boy hacked into a murderous lesson
recalled in me forever
like a lurch of earth on the edge of sleep
etched into my visions
food for dragonfish that learn
to live upon whatever they must eat
fused images beneath my pain.

II

The Pearl River floods through the streets of Jackson
A Mississippi summer televised.
Trapped houses kneel like sinners in the rain
a white woman climbs from her roof to a passing boat
her fingers tarry for a moment on the chimney
now awash
tearless and no longer young, she holds

a tattered baby's blanket in her arms.
In a flickering afterimage of the nightmare rain
a microphone
thrust up against her flat bewildered words
     "we jest come from the bank yestiddy
          borrowing money to pay the income tax
          now everything's gone. I never knew
          it could be so hard."
Despair weighs down her voice like Pearl River mud
caked around the edges
her pale eyes scanning the camera for help or explanation
unanswered
she shifts her search across the watered street, dry-eyed
        "hard, but not this hard."
Two tow-headed children hurl themselves against her
hanging upon her coat like mirrors
until a man with ham-like hands pulls her aside
snarling "She ain't got nothing more to say!"
and that lie hangs in his mouth
like a shred of rotting meat.

    III
I inherited Jackson, Mississippi.
For my majority it gave me Emmett Till
his 15 years puffed out like bruises
on plump boy-cheeks
his only Mississippi summer
whistling a 21 gun salute to Dixie
as a white girl passed him in the street
and he was baptized my son forever
in the midnight waters of the Pearl.

His broken body is the afterimage of my 21st year
when I walked through a northern summer
my eyes averted
from each corner's photographies
newspapers protest posters magazines
Police Story, Confidential, True
the avid insistence of detail
pretending insight or information
the length of gash across the dead boy's loins
his grieving mother's lamentation
the severed lips, how many burns
his gouged out eyes
sewed shut upon the screaming covers
louder than life
all over
the veiled warning, the secret relish
of a black child's mutilated body
fingered by street-corner eyes
bruise upon livid bruise
and wherever I looked that summer
I learned to be at home with children's blood
with savored violence
with pictures of black broken flesh
used, crumpled, and discarded
lying amid the sidewalk refuse
like a raped woman's face.

A black boy from Chicago
whistled on the streets of Jackson, Mississippi
testing what he'd been taught was a manly thing to do
his teachers

ripped his eyes out his sex his tongue
and flung him to the Pearl weighted with stone
in the name of white womanhood
they took their aroused honor
back to Jackson
and celebrated in a whorehouse
the double ritual of white manhood
confirmed.

IV
    "If earth and air and water do not judge them who are
    we to refuse a crust of bread?"

Emmett Till rides the crest of the Pearl, whistling
24 years his ghost lay like the shade of a raped woman
and a white girl has grown older in costly honor
(what did she pay to never know its price?)
now the Pearl River speaks its muddy judgment
and I can withhold my pity and my bread.

        "Hard, but not this hard."
Her face is flat with resignation and despair
with ancient and familiar sorrows
a woman surveying her crumpled future
as the white girl besmirched by Emmett's whistle
never allowed her own tongue
without power or conclusion
unvoiced
she stands adrift in the ruins of her honor
and a man with an executioner's face
pulls her away.

Within my eyes
the flickering afterimages of a nightmare rain
a woman wrings her hands
beneath the weight of agonies remembered
I wade through summer ghosts
betrayed by vision
hers and my own
becoming dragonfish to survive
the horrors we are living
with tortured lungs
adapting to breathe blood.

A woman measures her life's damage
my eyes are caves, chunks of etched rock
tied to the ghost of a black boy
whistling
crying and frightened
her tow-headed children cluster
like little mirrors of despair
their father's hands upon them
and soundlessly
a woman begins to weep.

[1981]

A Poem For Women In Rage

A killing summer heat wraps up the city
emptied of all who are not bound to stay
a black woman waits for a white woman
leans against the railing in the Upper Westside street
at intermission
the distant sounds of Broadway dim to lulling
until I can hear the voice of sparrows
like a promise I await
the woman I love
our slice of time
a place beyond the city's pain.

In the corner phonebooth a woman
glassed in by reflections of the street between us
her white face dangles
a tapestry of disasters seen
through a veneer of order
her mouth drawn like an ill-used roadmap
to eyes without core, a bottled heart
impeccable credentials of old pain.

The veneer cracks open
hate launches through the glaze into my afternoon
our eyes touch like hot wire
and the street snaps into nightmare
a woman with white eyes is clutching
a bottle of Fleischmann's gin
is fumbling at her waistband
is pulling a butcher knife from her ragged pants

her hand arcs backward "You Black Bitch!"
the heavy blade spins out toward me
slow motion
years of fury surge upward like a wall
I do not hear it
clatter to the pavement at my feet.

A gear of ancient nightmare churns
swift in familiar dread and silence
but this time I am awake, released
I smile. Now. This time is
my turn.
I bend to the knife my ears blood-drumming
across the street my lover's voice
the only moving sound within white heat
"Don't touch it!"
I straighten, weaken, then start down again
hungry for resolution
simple as anger and so close at hand
my fingers reach for the familiar blade
the known grip of wood against my palm
I have held it to the whetstone
a thousand nights for this
escorting fury through my sleep
like a cherished friend
to wake in the stink of rage
beside the sleep-white face of love

The keen steel of a dreamt knife
sparks honed from the whetted edge with a tortured shriek
between my lover's voice and the grey spinning
a choice of pain or fury

slashing across judgment like a crimson scar
I could open her up to my anger
with a point sharpened upon love.

In the deathland my lover's voice
fades
like the roar of a train derailed
on the other side of a river
every white woman's face I love
and distrust is upon it
eating green grapes from a paper bag
marking yellow exam-books tucked into a manilla folder
orderly as the last thought before death
I throw the switch.
Through screams of crumpled steel
I search the wreckage for a ticket of hatred
my lover's voice
calling
a knife at her throat.

In this steaming aisle of the dead
I am weeping
to learn the names of those streets
my feet have worn thin with running
and why they will never serve me
nor ever lead me home.
"Don't touch it!" she cries
I straighten myself
in confusion
a drunken woman is running away
down the Westside street

my lover's voice moves me
to a shadowy clearing.

Corralled in fantasy
the woman with white eyes has vanished
to become her own nightmare
a french butcher blade hangs in my house
love's token
I remember this knife
it carved its message into my sleeping
she only read its warning
written upon my face.

[1981]

from

Our Dead
Behind Us

(1986)

to
Gloria I. Joseph
tikoro nnko agyina [*]

---

[*] Ashanti proverb: "One head cannot go into counsel"

To the Poet Who Happens to Be Black and the Black Poet Who Happens to Be a Woman

I

I was born in the gut of Blackness
from between my mother's particular thighs
her waters broke upon blue-flowered lineoleum
and turned to slush in the Harlem cold
10 PM on a full moon's night
my head crested round as a clock
"You were so dark," my mother said
"I thought you were a boy."

II

The first time I touched my sister   alive
I was sure   the earth took note
but we were not new
false skin peeled off like gloves of fire
yoked flame   I was
stripped to the tips of my fingers
her song written into my palms my nostrils my belly
welcome home
in a language   I was pleased to relearn.

III

No cold spirit ever strolled through my bones
on the corner of Amsterdam Avenue
no dog mistook me for a bench
nor a tree   nor a bone

no lover envisioned my plump brown arms
as wings   nor misnamed me condor
but I can recall without counting
eyes
cancelling me out
like an unpleasant appointment
postage due
stamped in yellow   red   purple
any color
except Black   and choice
and woman
alive.

   IV
I cannot recall the words of my first poem
but I remember a promise
I made my pen
never to leave it
lying
in somebody else's blood.

Outlines

I

What hue lies in the slit of anger
ample and pure as night
what color the channel
blood comes through?

A Black woman and a white woman
charter our courses close
in a sea of calculated distance
warned away by reefs of hidden anger
histories rallied against us
the friendly face of cheap alliance.

Jonquils through the Mississippi snow
you entered my vision
with the force of hurled rock
defended by distance and a warning smile
fossil tears   pitched over the heart's wall
for protection
no other women
grown beyond safety
come back to tell us
whispering
past the turned shoulders
of our closest
we were not the first
Black woman white woman
altering course to fit our own journey.

———————

In this treacherous sea
even the act of turning
is almost fatally difficult
coming around full face
into a driving storm
putting an end to running
before the wind.

On a helix of white
the letting of blood
the face of my love
and rage
coiled in my brown arms
an ache in the bone
we cannot alter history
by ignoring it
nor the contradictions
who we are.

II
A Black woman and a white woman
in the open fact of our loving
with not only our enemies' hands
raised against us
means a gradual sacrifice
of all that is simple
dreams
where you walk the mountain
still as a water-spirit
your arms lined with scalpels
and I hide the strength of my hungers
like a throwing knife in my hair.

Guilt wove through quarrels like barbed wire
fights in the half forgotten schoolyard
gob of spit in a childhood street
yet both our mothers once scrubbed kitchens
in houses where comfortable women
died a separate silence
our mothers' nightmares
trapped into familiar hatred
the convenience of others drilled into their lives
like studding into a wall
they taught us to understand
only the strangeness of men.

To give   but not beyond what is wanted
to speak   as well as to bear
the weight of hearing
Fragments of the word wrong
clung to my lashes like ice
confusing my vision with a crazed brilliance
your face   distorted into grids
of magnified complaint
our first winter
we made a home outside of symbol
learned to drain the expansion tank together
to look beyond the agreed-upon disguises
not to cry each other's tears.

How many Februarys
shall I lime this acid soil
inch by inch
reclaimed through our gathered waste?
from the wild onion shoots of April

to mulch in the August sun
squash blossoms   a cement driveway
kale and tomatoes
muscles etch the difference
between I need and forever.

When we first met
I had never been
for a walk in the woods

   III
light catches two women on a trail
together   embattled by choice
carving an agenda with tempered lightning
and no certainties
we mark tomorrow
examining every cell of the past
for what is useful   stoked by furies
we were supposed to absorb by forty
still we grow   more precise with each usage
like falling stars or torches
we print code names upon the scars
over each other's resolutions
our weaknesses   no longer hateful.

When women make love
beyond the first exploration
we meet each other   knowing
in a landscape
the rest of our lives
attempts to understand.

IV

Leaf-dappled the windows lighten
after a battle that leaves our night in tatters
and we two glad to be alive   and tender
the outline of your ear pressed on my shoulder
keeps a broken dish from becoming always.

We rise to dogshit   dumped on our front porch
the brass windchimes from Sundance stolen
despair offerings of the 8 A.M. News
reminding us we are still at war
and not with each other
"give us 22 minutes and we will give you the world . . ."
and still we dare
to say we are committed
sometimes without relish.

Ten blocks down the street
a cross is burning
we are a Black woman and a white woman
with two Black children
you talk with our next-door neighbors
I register for a shotgun
we secure the tender perennials
against an early frost
reconstructing a future we fuel
from our living   different precisions
In the next room a canvas chair
whispers beneath your weight
a breath of you between laundered towels
the flinty places that do not give.

V

Your face upon my shoulder
a crescent of freckle over bone
what we share   illuminates what we do not
the rest is a burden of history
we challenge
bearing each bitter piece to the light
we hone ourselves upon each other's courage
loving
as we cross the mined bridge   fury
tuned like a Geiger counter

to the softest place.
One straight light hair on the washbasin's rim
difference
intimate as a borrowed scarf
the children arrogant as mirrors
our pillows' mingled scent
this grain of our particular days
keeps a fine sharp edge
to which I cling like a banner
in a choice of winds
seeking an emotional language
in which to abbreviate time.

I trace the curve of your jaw
with a lover's finger
knowing the hardest battle
is only the first
how to do what we need for our living
with honor and in love
we have chosen each other

and the edge of each other's battles
the war is the same
if we lose
someday women's blood will congeal
upon a dead planet
if we win
there is no telling.

Equal Opportunity

The american deputy assistant secretary of defense
for Equal Opportunity
and safety
is a home girl.
Blindness slashes our tapestry to shreds.

The moss-green military tailoring sets off her color
beautifully
she says "when I stand up to speak in uniform
you can believe everyone takes notice!"
Superimposed skull-like across her trim square shoulders
dioxin-smear
the stench of napalm upon growing cabbage
the chug and thud of Corsairs in the foreground
advance like a blush across her cheeks
up the unpaved road outside Grenville, Grenada

An M–16 bayonet gleams
slashing away the wooden latch
of a one-room slat house in Soubise
mopping up   weapons search   pockets of resistance
Imelda   young   Black   in a tattered headcloth
standing to one side on her left foot
takes notice
one wrist behind her hip the other
palm-up beneath her chin   watching
armed men in moss-green jumpsuits turn out her shack
watching   mashed-up nutmeg trees
the trampled cocoa pods

graceless broken stalks of almost ripe banana
her sister has been missing now ten days

Beside the shattered waterpipe downroad
Granny Lou's consolations
> *If it was only kill*
> *they'd wanted to kill we*
> *many more would have died*
> *look at Lebanon*
> *so as wars go this was an easy one*
> *But for we here*
> *who never woke up before*
> *to see plane shitting fire into chimney*
> *it was a damn awful lot!*

The baby's father buried without his legs
burned bones in piles along the road
"any Cubans around here, girl? any guns?"
singed tree-ferns curl and jerk in the mortar rhythms
strumming up from shore   uphill a tree explodes
showering the house with scraps of leaves
the sweetish smell of unseen rotting flesh.

For a while there was almost enough
water   enough rice   enough quinine
the child tugs at her waistband
but she does not move quickly
she has heard how nervous these green men are
with their grenades and sweaty helmets
who offer cigarettes and chocolate but no bread
free batteries and herpes but no doctors
no free buses to the St. Georges market

no reading lessons in the brilliant afternoons
bodies strewn along Telescope Beach
these soldiers say are foreigners
but she has seen the charred bits of familiar cloth
and knows what to say to any invader
with an M–16 rifle held ready
while searching her cooking shed
overturning the empty pots with his apologetic grin
Imelda steps forward
the child pressing against her knees
"no guns, man, no guns here. we glad you come. you carry
water?"

The american deputy assistant secretary of defense
for equal opportunity and safety
pauses in her speech   licks her dry lips
"as you can see the Department has
a very good record
of equal opportunity for our women"
swims toward safety
through a lake of her own blood.

Diaspora

Afraid is a country with no exit visas
a wire of ants walking the horizon
embroiders our passports at birth
Johannesburg Alabama
a dark girl flees the cattle prods
skin hanging from her shredded nails
escapes into my nightmare
half an hour before the Shatila dawn
wakes in the well of a borrowed Volkswagen
or a rickety midnight sleeper out of White River Junction
Washington bound   again
gulps carbon monoxide in a false-bottomed truck
fording the Braceras Grande
or an up-country river
grenades held dry in a calabash
leaving.

A Question of Climate

I learned to be honest
the way I learned to swim
dropped into the inevitable
my father's thumbs in my hairless armpits
about to give way
I am trying
to surface   carefully
remembering
the water's shadow-legged musk
cannons of salt   exploding
my nostrils' rage
and for years
my powerful breast stroke
was a declaration of war.

Florida

Black people fishing the causeway
full-skirted   bare brown to the bellyband
atilt on the railing   near a concrete road
where a crawler-transporter will move
the space shuttle from hangar to gantry.

Renting a biplane to stalk the full moon in Aquarius
as she rose under Venus between propellers Country Western surf
feasting on frozen black beans Cubano from Grand Union
in the mangrove swamp   elbows of cypress   scrub oak

Moon   moon   moon on the syncopated road
rimey with bullfrogs   walking beaches   fragrant and raunchy
fire-damp sand between my toes.

Huge arrogant cockroaches   with white people's manners
and their palmetto bug cousins
aggressive ridged slowness
the obstinacy of living fossils.

Sweet ugly-fruit   avocados   tomatoes
and melon in the mango slot
hibiscus spread like a rainbow of lovers
arced stamens waving
but even the jacaranda only last a day.

Crescent moon walking my sheets at midnight
lonely in the palmetto thicket   counting
persistent Canaveral lizards launch themselves

through my air conditioner
chasing equally determined fleas.

In Gainesville the last time there was only one
sister present who said   "I'm gonna remember your name
and the next time you come there'll be
quite a few more of us, hear?"
and there certainly was   a warm pool
of dark women's faces
in the sea of listening.

The first thing I did when I got home
after kissing my honey
was to wash my hair with small flowers
and begin a five-day fast.

Political Relations

In a hotel in Tashkent
the Latvian delegate from Riga
was sucking his fishbones
as a Chukwu woman with hands as hot as mine
caressed my knee beneath the dinner table
her slanted eyes were dark as seal fur
we did not know each other's tongue.

"Someday we will talk through our children"
she said
"I spoke to your eyes this morning
you have such a beautiful face"
thin-lipped Moscow girls translated for us
smirking at each other.

And I had watched her in the Conference Hall
ox-solid   black electric hair
straight as a deer's rein   fire-disc eyes
sweeping over the faces
like a stretch of frozen tundra
we were two ends of one taut rope
stretched like a promise from her mouth
singing the friendship song
her people sang for greeting
> There are only fourteen thousand of us left
> it is a very sad thing   it is a very sad thing
> when any people   any people   dies

———

"Yes, I heard you this morning"
I said   reaching out from the place where we touched
poured her vodka   an offering
which she accepted like roses
leaning across our white Russian interpreters
to kiss me softly upon my lips.

Then she got up and left
with the Latvian delegate from Riga.

There Are No Honest Poems About Dead Women

What do we want from each other
after we have told our stories
do we want
to be healed   do we want
mossy quiet stealing over our scars
do we want
the powerful unfrightening sister
who will make the pain go away
mother's voice   in the hallway
you've done it right
the first time   darling
you will never need
to do it again.

Thunder grumbles on the horizon
I buy time with another story
a pale blister of air
cadences of dead flesh
obscure the vowels.

from

The Marvelous Arithmetics of Distance

(1993)

*To My Sister Pat Parker, Poet and
Comrade-in-Arms In Memoriam*

*and to my blood sisters
Mavis Jones
Marjorie Jones
Phyllis Blackwell
Helen Lorde*

Making Love to Concrete

An upright abutment in the mouth
of the Willis Avenue bridge
a beige Honda leaps the divider
like a steel gazelle   inescapable
sleek leather boots on the pavement
rat-a-tat-tat   best intentions
going down for the third time
stuck   in the particular

You cannot make love to concrete
if you care about being
non-essential   wrong or worn   thin
if you fear ever becoming
diamonds or lard
you cannot make love to concrete
if you cannot pretend
concrete needs your loving

To make love to concrete
you need an indelible feather
white dresses before you are ten
a confirmation lace veil   milk-large bones
and air raid drills in your nightmares
no stars till you go to the country
and one summer when you are twelve
Con Edison pulls the plug
on the street-corner moons   Walpurgisnacht
and there are sudden new lights in the sky
stone chips that forget   you need

to become a light rope   a hammer
a repeatable bridge
garden-fresh broccoli   two dozen dropped
   eggs
and a hint of you

Thaw

The language of past seasons
collapses   pumpkins in spring
false labor slides like mud
off the face of ease
and whatever I turn my hand to
pales in the sun.

We will always be there to your call
the old witches said
always said   always saying
something else   at the same time
you are trapped   asleep
you are speechless
perhaps   you will also be
broken.

Step lightly   all around us
words are cracking
off   we drift
separate and syllabic
if we survive at all.

Inheritance—His

I

My face resembles your face
less and less each day. When I was young
no one mistook whose child I was.
Features   build   coloring
alone among my creamy fine-boned sisters
marked me Byron's daughter.

No sun set when you died, but a door
opened onto my mother. After you left
she grieved her crumpled world aloft
an iron fist sweated with business symbols
a printed blotter   *dwell in a house of Lord's*
your hollow voice chanting down a hospital corridor
   yea, though I walk through the valley
   of the shadow of death
   I will fear no evil.

II

I rummage through the deaths you lived
swaying on a bridge of question.
At seven   in Barbados
dropped into your unknown father's life
your courage vault from his tailor's table
back to the sea
Did the Grenada treeferns sing
your 15th summer as you jumped ship
to seek your mother

finding her   too late
surrounded with new sons?

Who did you bury to become enforcer of the law
the handsome legend
before whose raised arm even trees wept
a man of deep and wordless passion
who wanted sons and got five girls?
You left the first two scratching in a treefern's shade
the youngest is a renegade poet
searching for your answer in my blood.

My mother's Grenville tales
spin through early summer evenings.
But you refused to speak of home
of stepping proud Black and penniless
into this land where only white men
ruled by money.   How you labored
in the docks of the Hotel Astor
your bright wife a chambermaid upstairs
welded love and survival to ambition
as the land of promise withered
crashed   the hotel closed
and you peddle dawn-bought apples
from a pushcart on Broadway.
Does an image of return
wealthy and triumphant
warm your childblained fingers
as you count coins in the Manhattan snow
or is it only Linda
who dreams of home?

When my mother's first-born crys for milk
in the brutal city winter
do the faces of your other daughters dim
like the image of the treeferned yard
where a dark girl first cooked for you
and her ash heap still smells curry?

III

Did the secret of my sisters steal your tongue
like I stole money from your midnight pockets
stubborn and quaking
as you threaten to shoot me if I am the one?
the naked lightbulbs in our kitchen ceiling
glint off your service revolver
as you load   whispering.
Did two little dark girls in Grenada
dart like flying fish
between your averred eyes
and my pajamaless body
our last adolescent summer
eavesdropped orations
to your shaving mirror
our most intense conversations
were you practicing how to tell me
of my twin sisters   abandoned
as you had been abandoned
by another Black woman seeking
her fortune   Grenada   Barbados
Panama   Grenada.
New York City.

IV

You bought old books at auction
for my unlanguaged world
gave me your idols   Marcus Garvey   Citizen Kane
and morsels from your dinner plate
when I was seven.
I owe you my Dahomeyan jaw
the free high school for gifted girls
no one else thought I should attend
and the darkness that we share.
Our deepest bonds remain
the mirror and the gun.

V

An elderly Black judge
known for his way with women
visits this island where I live
shakes my hand, smiling
"I knew your father," he says
"quite a man!" Smiles again.
I flinch at his raised eyebrow.
A long-gone woman's voice
lashes out at me   in parting
"You will never be satisfied
until you have the whole world
in your bed!"

Now I am older than you were when you died
overwork and silence exploding in your brain.
You are gradually receding from my face.
Who were you outside the 23rd Psalm?
Knowing so little

how did I become so much
like you?

Your hunger for rectitude
blossoms into rage
the hot tears of mourning
never shed for you before
your twisted measurements
the agony of denial
the power of unshared secrets.

[January 23–September 10, 1992]

jessehelms

I am a Black woman
writing my way to the future
off a garbage scow knit from moral fiber
stuck together with jessehelms'
come   where Art is a dirty word
scrawled on the wall
of Bilbo's memorial outhouse
and obscenity is catching
even I'd like to hear you scream
ream out your pussy
with my dildo called Nicaragua
ram Grenada up your fighole
till Panama runs out of you
like Savimbi aflame.

But you prefer to do it
on the senate floor
amid a sackful of paper pricks
keeping time to a 195 million dollar
military band
safe-sex dripping from your tongue
into avid senatorial ears.

Later you'll get yours
behind the senate toilets
where they're waiting for you jessehelms
those white boys with their pendulous rules
bumping against the rear door of Europe

spread-eagled across the globe
their crystal balls poised over Africa
ass-up for old glory.

Your turn now jessehelms
come on its time
to lick the handwriting
off the walls.

The Politics of Addiction

17 luxury condominiums
electronically protected
from criminal hunger   the homeless
seeking a night's warmth
across from the soup kitchen
St. Vincent's Hospital
razor wire covering the hot air grates.
Disrobed need
shrieks through the nearby streets.

Some no longer beg.
a brown sloe-eyed boy
picks blotches from his face
eyes my purse shivering
white dust a holy fire
in his blood
at the corner   fantasy
parodies desire   replaces longing
Green light.   The boy turns back
to the steaming grates.

Down the street in a show-window
camera   Havana
the well-shaped woman smiles
waves her plump arm along
half-filled market shelves
excess expectation
dusts across her words

*"Si hubieran capitalismo
hubiesen tomates aquí!"*
"If we had capitalism
tomatoes would be here now."

Today Is Not the Day

I can't just sit here
staring death in her face
blinking and asking for a new name
by which to greet her

I am not afraid to say
unembellished
I am dying
but I do not want to do it
looking the other way.

Today is not the day.
It could be
but it is not.
Today is today
in the early moving morning
sun shining down upon
the farmhouse in my belly
lighting the wellswept alleys
of the town growing in my liver
intricate vessels swelling with the gift
of Mother Mawu
or her mischievous daughter
Afrekete   Afrekete   my beloved
feel the sun of my days surround you
binding our pathways
we have water to carry
honey to harvest
bright seed to plant for the next fair

we will linger
exchanging sweet oil
along each other's ashy legs
the evening light
a crest on your cheekbones.

By this rising
some piece of our labor
is already half-done
the taste of loving
doing a bit of work
having some fun
riding my wheels so close to the line
my eyelashes blaze.

Beth dangles her stethoscope over the rearview mirror
Jonathan fine-tunes his fix on Orion
working through another equation
youth taut as an arrow
stretched to their borders
the barb sinking in so far
it vanishes from the surface.
I dare not tremble for them
only pray laughter comes often enough
to soften the edge.

And Gloria   Gloria
whose difference I learn
with the love of a sister   you   you
in my eyes bright appetite   light
playing along your muscle
as you swing.

This could be the day.
I could slip anchor and wander
to the end of the jetty
uncoil into the waters
a vessel of light   moonglade
ride the freshets to sundown
and when I am gone
another stranger will find you
coiled on the warm sand
beached treasure   and love you
for the different stories
your seas tell
and half-finished blossoms
growing out of my season
trail behind
with a comforting hum.

But today
is not the day.
Today.

[April 22, 1992]

Notes

"Poetry Is Not a Luxury"
First published in *Chrysalis: A Magazine of Female Culture*, no. 3 (1977).

"The Transformation of Silence into Language and Action"
Paper delivered at the Modern Language Association's Lesbian and Literature Panel, Chicago, Illinois, December 28, 1977. First published in *Sinister Wisdom* 6 (1978) and *The Cancer Journals* (San Francisco: Spinsters Ink, 1980).

"My Mother's Mortar"
This version of the essay was first published in *Sinister Wisdom* 8 (1977): 54–61.

"Uses of the Erotic"
Paper delivered at the Fourth Berkshire Conference on the History of Women, Mount Holyoke College, August 25, 1978. First published as a pamphlet by Out & Out Books. Now published as a pamphlet by Kore Press.

"The Master's Tools Will Never Dismantle the Master's House"
Comments at the Personal and the Political Panel, Second Sex Conference, New York, September 29, 1979.

"Sexism"
First published as "The Great American Disease" in *The Black Scholar* 10, no. 9 (May–June 1979) in response to "The Myth of

Black Macho: A Response to Angry Black Feminists" by Robert Staples in *The Black Scholar* 10, no. 8 (March–April 1979).

"The Uses of Anger"

Keynote presentation at the National Women's Studies Association Conference, Storrs, Connecticut, June 1981.

"Fourth of July"

Excerpted from *Zami: A New Spelling of My Name – A Biomythology* (Watertown, MA: Persephone Press, 1982; Trumansburg, NY: Crossing Press / Penguin Random House, 1983).

"I Am Your Sister"

First published in pamphlet form along with "Apartheid U.S.A." (Kitchen Table: Women of Color Press, 1985). Subsequently published in *A Burst of Light: Essays by Audre Lorde* (Ithaca, NY: Firebrand Books, 1988).

"A Burst of Light: Living with Cancer"

First published in *A Burst of Light: Essays by Audre Lorde* (Ithaca, NY: Firebrand Books, 1988).

"Is Your Hair Still Political?"

Audre Lorde Papers, Box 8, Spelman College Archives. Subsequently published in *Go Girl! The Black Woman's Book of Travel and Adventure*, ed. Elaine Lee (Portland, OR: Eighth Mountain Press, 1997).

"Difference and Survival"

Undated address, Audre Lorde Papers, Box 8, Spelman College Archives. First published in *I Am Your Sister: Collected and Unpublished Writings of Audre Lorde*, ed. Rudolph P. Byrd, Johnnetta Betsch Cole, and Beverly Guy-Sheftall (New York: Oxford University Press, 2009).

Prose Index

Poetry Index